General Knowledge

ABBREVIATIONS

A

A.A.F.	Auxiliary Air Force
A.A.S.U.	All Assam Students Union
A.C.D.	Asian Co-operation Dialogue
A.D.B.	Asian Development Bank
A.E.C.	Atomic Energy Commission
A.F.P.R.O.	Action for Food Production
A.I.C.C.	All India Congress Committee
A.I.D.W.A.	All India Democratic Women's Association
A.I.D.S.	Acquired Immune Deficiency Syndrome
A.I.H.B.	All India Handicrafts Board
A.I.R.	Annual Information Report
A.J.T.	Advanced Jet Trainer
A.P.E.C.	Asia-Pacific Economic Cooperation
A.R.F.	ASEAN Regional Forum
A.S.E.A.N.	Association of South-East Asian Nations
A.S.L.V.	Augmented Satellite Launch Vehicle
A.T.M.	Automated Teller Machine
A.U.	African Union
A.E.S.	Acute Encephalitis Syndrome
A.W.A.N.	Army Wide Area Network
A.Y.U.S.H.	Ayurveda, Yoga and Naturopathy, Unani, Siddha and Homeopathy

B

B.A.R.C.	Bhabha Atomic Research Centre
B.C.C.I.	Board of Control of Cricket in India/Bank of Credit and Commerce International
B.C.G.	Bacille Calmette Guerin (Anti-T.B. vaccine)
B.B.C.	British Broadcasting Corporation
B.C.T.T.	Banking Cash Transaction Tax
B.O.A.C.	British Overseas Airways Corporation
B.P.O.	Business Process Outsourcing
BREAD	Basic Research Education And Development (SOCIETY)
B.S.N.L.	Bharat Sanchar Nigam Ltd.
B.V.R.A.A.M.	Beyond Visual Range Air-to-Air Missile

C

C.A.	Chartered Accountant
C.A.A.	Citizenship Amendment Act
C.A.C.	Capital Account Convertibility
C.A.C.C.I.	Confederation of Asia-Pacific Chambers of Commerce and Industry

C.A.C.P.	Commission for Agriculture Costs and Prices
C.B.Ms	Confidence Building Measures
C.C.I.	Cricket Club of India, Consumer Confidence Index
C.D.M.A.	Code Division Multiple Access
C.F.S.I.	Children's Film Society India
C.F.L.	Compact Fluorescent Lamps
C.G.I.A.R.	Consultative Group on International Agricultural Research
C.H.O.G.M.	Commonwealth Heads of Government Meeting
C.I.A.	Central Intelligence Agency (U.S.A.)
C.I.C.	Chief Information Commissioner
CITES	The Convention on International Trade in Endangered Species of Wild Fauna and Flora.
C.M.P.	The Common Minimum Programme
C.N.G.	Compressed Natural Gas
C.O.F.E.P.O.S.A.	The Conservation of Foreign Exchange and Prevention of Smuggling Activities Act
C.F.C.	Common Fund for Commodities
C.P.I.	Corruption Perception Index, Consumer Price Index.
C.R.I.S.I.L.	Credit Rating and Information Services of India Ltd.
CRY	Child Rights and You
C.S.I.R.	Council of Scientific and Industrial Research
C.S.C.A.P.	Council for Security Co-operation in the Asia Pacific

D

D.A.	Dearness Allowances
D.A.E.	Department of Atomic Energy
D.A.S.A.	Direct Admission of Students Abroad
D.D.T.	Dichloro-diphenyl Trichloro-ethane
D.M.R.C.	Delhi Metro Rail Corporation
D.Litt.	Doctor of Literature
D.O.T.S.	Directly Observed Treatment Short Course (For Tuberculosis)
D.R.D.O.	Defence Research and Development Organisation

E

E.A.S.	East Asia Summit
E.C.G.C.	Export Credit Guarantee Corporation
e.g.	exempli gratia (For Example)
E.P.F.O.	Employees' Provident Fund Organisation
E.S.C.A.P.	Economic & Social Commission for Asia and the Pacific (This is the new name of ECAFE)
E.V.M.	Electronic Voting Machine

F

F.A.O.	Food and Agriculture Organisation
F.D.I.	Foreign Direct Investment
FEMA	Foreign Exchange of India Management Act
F.I.C.A.	Federation of International Cricketers Association
F.I.U.I.	Finance Intelligence Unit of India

G

G.A.T.T.	General Agreement on Tariffs and Trade
G.D.P.	Gross Domestic Product
Ge.S.C.I.	Global e-School and Communities Initiative
G.N.H.	Gross National Happiness
G.P.R.S.	General Packet Radio Service
G.S.O.	Geo-Stationary Orbit
G.S.T.	Goods and Service Tax

H

H.E.I.C.	Honourable East India Company
H.M.T.	Hindustan Machine Tools
H.U.D.C.O.	Housing and Urban Development Corporation

I

I.A.A.I.	International Airport Authority of India
I.A.A.F.	International Amateur Athletic Federation
I.B.A.C.	International Business Advisory Council
I.B.S.A.	India, Brazil, South Africa.
I.C.R.C.	International Committee of the Red Cross
I.C.R.I.E.R.	Indian Council for Research on International Economic Relations
I.D.B.I.	Industrial Development Bank of India
I.G.C.A.R.	Indira Gandhi Centre for Atomic Research
I.F.W.J.	Indian Federation of Working Journalists
I.G.M.D.P.	Integrated Guided Missile Development Programme
I.G.N.C.A.	Indira Gandhi National Centre for Arts
INSDOC	Indian National Scientific Documentation Centre
I.N.T.U.C.	Indian National Trade Union Congress
I.C.A.R.	Indian Council of Agricultural Research
I.C.C.	International Cricket Council
I.D.A.	International Development Association
I.L.O.	International Labour Organisation
I.M.F.	International Monetary Fund
I.N.A.	Indian National Army
I.N.M.A.S.	Institute of Nuclear Medicines and Allied Sciences

I.N.S.	Indian News Paper Society, Indian Navy Ship
I.P.O.	Initial Public Offering
I.R.N.S.S.	The Indian Regional Navigation Satellite System
I.S.B.	Indian School of Business
I.S.I.	Inter Services Intelligence (Pakistan)
I.S.T.	Indian Standard Time
I.S.R.O.	Indian Space Research Organisation
I.T.P.O.	India Trade Promotion Organisation
I.U.C.N.	International Union for Conservation of Nature

L

LL.B.	Bachelor of Legislative Law (Bachelor of Laws)
L.E.D.	Light Emitting Diode
L.P.G.	Liquefied Petroleum Gas

M

M.B.B.S.	Bachelor of Medicine and Bachelor of Surgery
M.C.C.	Marylebone Cricket Club
M.D.M.K.	Marumalarchi Dravida Munnetra Kazhagam.
MESSENGER	Mercury Surface, Space, Environment, Geochemistry and Ranging (Mission)
M.F.A.L.A.	Marginal Farmers and Agricultural Labour Agency
M.N.N.A.	Major Non-Nato Ally
M.T.A.	Multirole Transport Aircraft

N

N.A.C.O.	National Aids Control Organisation
N.A.T.O.	North Atlantic Treaty Organisation
N.C.A.	National Cricket Academy
N.C.A.	Nuclear Command Authority
N.C.A.O.R.	National Centre for Antarctic and Ocean Research
N.C.S.C.	National Commission for Scheduled Castes
N.D.A.	National Democratic Alliance
N.D.C.	National Development Council
N.D.I.C.	Natural Disaster Information System
N.D.M.A.	National Disaster Management Authority
N.E.A.	National Environment Agency
N.F.F.W.P.	National Food for Work Programme
N.G.T.	National Green Tribunal
N.I.A.S.	National Institute of Advanced Studies
N.I.T.I.	*National Institution for Transforming India*
N.K.C.	National Knowledge Commission

N.O.T.A.	None of the Above
N.L.L.M.	National Legal Literacy Mission
N.R.C.	National Register of Citizens
N.R.E.G.S.	National Rural Employment Guarantee Scheme
N.R.H.M.	National Rural Health Mission
N.S.G.	National Security Guards; Nuclear Suppliers' Group

O

O.I.G.S.	On Indian Government Service
OIL	Oil India Limited
O.M.R.	Optical Mark Reader/Recognition
O.N.G.C.	Oil and Natural Gas Commission
O.P.E.C.	Organisation of Petroleum Exporting Countries

P

P.A.C.	Public Accounts Committee, Provincial Armed Constabulary, Professional Aptitude Council, Parliamentary Affairs Committee
P.E.T.A.	People to the Ethical Treatment of Animals
P.F.R.D.A.	Pension Fund Regulatory and Development Authority
P.H.D.C.C.I.	Progress, Harmony and Development Chambers of Commerce and Industry
P.I.N.	Personal Identity Number
PIN Code	Postal Index Number Code
P.M.E.G.P.	Prime Minister's Employment Generation Programme
POTA	Prevention of Terrorism Act
P.P.I.	Professionals' Party of India
P.U.R.A.	Providing Urban Amenities in Rural Areas
P.W.G.	Peoples War Group

R

R.A.F.	Rapid Action Force
R.E.C.	Rural Electrification Corporation
R.G.I.P.T.	Rajiv Gandhi Institute of Petroleum Technology
R.T.R.A.	Rail Tariff Regulatory Authority

S

S.A.F.M.A.	South Asia Free Media Association
S.A.S.E.	Self Addressed Stamped Envelop
S.A.R.S.	Severe Acute Respiratory Syndrome
S.A.H.R.	South Asian Human Rights Forum
S.A.S.S.	Sri Amarnath Sangharsh Samiti

S.C.O.	Shanghai Cooperation Organisation
S.E.Z.	Special Economic Zone
S.F.C.	Strategic Forces Command
S.G.R.Y.	Sampoorna Grameen Rojgar Yojana
S.I.M.	Subscriber Identification Module
S.M.S.	Short Message Service; Subscriber Management System.
S.P.A.	Seven Party Alliance
S.P.I.C.	Special Photo Identity Card
S.S.A.	Sarva Shiksha Abhiyan

T

TELCO	Tata Engineering and Locomotive Company Ltd.
T.E.R.L.S.	Thumba Equatorial Rocket Launching Station
T.R.I.B.	Temple Records Index Bureau

U

U.A.P.A.	Unlawful Activities (Prevention) Act.
U.C.C.	Uniform Civil Code
U.G.C.	University Grants Commission
U.N.E.S.C.O.	United Nations Educational Scientific and Cultural Organisation
U.N.D.F.	United Nations Democracy Fund
U.N.E.P.	United Nations Environment Programme
U.N.F.P.A.	United Nations Fund for Population Activities
U.N.I.C.E.F.	United Nations International Children's Emergency Fund
U.N.I.D.O.	United Nations Industrial Development Organisation
U.N.I.F.I.L.	United Nations Interim Force in Lebanon
U.N.M.O.V.I.C.	United Nations Monitoring, Verification and Inspection Commission
U.N.P.A.	United National Progressive Alliance, United Nations Postal Administration
U.P.A.	United Progressive Alliance

V

V.A.A.	Virgin Atlantic Airways Ltd., Value Added Agriculture
V.A.T.	Value Added Tax
VISTA	Volunteers in Service to America
V.P.P.	Value Payable Post
V.R.S.	*Voluntary Retirement* Scheme
V.S.S.C.	Vikram Sarabhai Space Centre

W

W.A.D.A.	World Anti-Doping Agency
W.A.P.	Wheel and Axle Plant
W.B.E.R.	World Bank Economic Review
W.C.A.R.	World Conference Against Racism
W.C.C.B.	Wildlife Crime Control Bureau
W.C.L.	Western Coalfields Limited
W.E.F.	World Environment Forum
W.F.D.B.	World Federation of Diamond Bourses
W.H.O.	World Health Organisation
WIPO	World Intellectual Property Organisation
W.L.L.	Wireless in a Local Loop
W.M.D.	Weapons of Mass Destruction
W.T.O.	World Tourism Organisation; World Trade Organisation
W.W.F.	World Wildlife Fund; War Wounded Foundation
W.W.W.	World Wide Web
WiFi	Wireless Fidelity

Y

Y.M.C.A.	Young Men's Christian Association
Y.W.C.A.	Young Women's Christian Association

Z

Z.S.	Zoological Society
Z.C.C.	Zonal Cultural Centres

SPORTS

CUPS AND TROPHIES (INDIA AND WORLD)

Agha Khan Cup	— Hockey
Barna Bellack Cup	— Table Tennis (Men)
Davis Cup	— Lawn Tennis (International)
Durand Cup	— Football (India)
Duleep Trophy	— Cricket (India)
Ezra Cup	— Polo
I.F.A. Shield	— Football
Jules Rimet Trophy	— Football (World)
Lady Ratan Tata Trophy	— Hockey (Women, India)
Ranji Trophy	— Cricket (India)
Rangaswami Cup	— National Hockey Championship India
Rohinton Baria Trophy	— Cricket (Inter-university)
Rovers Cup	— Football
Rene Frank Cup	— Hockey (India)
Swaythling Cup	— World Table Tennis (Men)
Santosh Trophy	— National Football (India)
Thomas Cup	— World Badminton (Men)
Walker Cup	— Golf
Wightman Cup	— Lawn Tennis (England)
Wimbledon Trophy	— Lawn Tennis (England)
Sudirman Cup	— Badminton
UEFA-Euro Cup	— Football
Indian Premier League	— Cricket
Sultan Azlan Shah Cup	— Hockey
Wimbledon Open	— Tennis
Laver Cup	— Tennis
Copa America Cup	— Football
Uber Cup	— Badminton (Women)

22nd Commonwealth Games

The 2022 Commonwealth Games, officially known as XXII Commonwealth Games or Birmingham (England), *were organised at Birmingham between 28th July to 8th August, 2022.* More than 5,034 athletes from 20 games took part. 23rd Commonwealth Game 2026 are proposed in Victoria (Australia).

XXII Commonwealth Games Medal Table : Top Ten Countries					
Sr. No.	**Country**	**Gold**	**Silver**	**Bronze**	**Total**
1.	Australia	67	57	54	178
2.	England	57	66	53	176
3.	Canada	26	32	34	92
4.	India	22	16	23	61
5.	New Zealand	20	12	17	49
6.	Scotland	13	11	27	51
7.	Nigeria	12	9	14	35
8.	Wales	8	6	14	28
9.	South Africa	7	9	11	27
10.	Malaysia	7	8	8	23

37th National Games (2023)

Host City—Goa, 26th Oct.–9th Nov., 2023
Events—43
Motto—Get Set Goa.
Mascot—Moga (Indian Bison)
Anthem—Khel
Raja Bhalindra Singh Trophy—Maharashtra.

National Games 2023 Medals Table					
Rank	**State/Union Territory/Team**	**Gold**	**Silver**	**Bronze**	**Total**
1	Maharashtra	67	61	65	193
2	Services	52	22	28	102
3	Haryana	48	33	47	128
4	Karnataka	28	23	25	76
5	Manipur	25	19	22	66
6	Madhya Pradesh	24	31	29	84
7	Delhi	19	17	46	82
8	Tamil Nadu	17	20	24	61
9	Kerala	15	19	21	55
10	Uttar Pradesh	11	19	22	52

- 38th National Games (2024) will be held in Uttarakhand.

Olympic Games

The history of Olympic Games is about twenty eight hundred years old. First of all these games were held by the Greeks in 776 B.C. on Mount Olympus in honour of the Greek god, Zeus. These games continued to be held every four years until 394 A.D. when they were stopped by a royal order of the emperor of Rome. These games were revived in 1894 by the efforts of a French Baron Pierre de Coubertin and the First Olympic meet in the modern series was held in 1896 in Athens, the capital of Greece. The 21st Olympic Games were held in 1976 at Montreal (Canada), the 22nd Olympic Games were held in 1980 in Moscow (USSR), the 23rd Olympic Games were held at Los Angeles (U.S.A.), in 1984, and the 24th Olympics were held from Sept.

17 to Oct. 2, 1988 at Seoul. The Mascot of the 24th Olympics was 'Hodori'. The 25th Olympic Games were held at Barcelona (Spain) in 1992 and 26th Olympic games were held from July 19 to Aug. 4, 1996 at Atlanta (U.S.A.). The Mascot of 25th Olympic games was Cobi. The Mascot of 26th Olympics was Iszi Atlanta '96. 27th Olympic Games were held in Sydney (Australia) in 2000 from Sept. 15 to Oct. 1. The Mascot of the 27th Olympics was a trio of Syd, Millie and Olly. At this first Olympiad of the new millennium, the largest number of medals were bagged by the U.S.A. followed by Russia. China was placed third. India bagged only one bronze medal. The twenty eighth Olympics were held at Athens (Greece) from August 13 to August 29, 2004. The Mascot of the 28th Olympics was a duo of Athena' and Phevos. The 29th Olympic Games were held in Beijing (China) from August 8 to August 24, 2008. The 30th Olympic Games were held in London from July 12, 2012. The 31st Olympic games were held in Rio de Janeiro in July 2016.

33rd Paris Olympic Games

The 2024 Summer Olympics, officially the Games of the XXXIII Olympiad, and also more generally known as Paris 2024, was a major international multi-sport event, celebrated in the tradition of the Olympic Games, as governed by the International Olympic Committee (IOC), that took place in Paris, from July 26 to August 11, 2024. As per Medal Tally, USA clinched the largest number of gold medals (40) followed by China (40) and Japan (20).

List of Medal Winners

1. Manu Bhaker; Medal—Bronze; *Event*—Women's 10 m Air Pistol.
2. Sarabjot Singh; Medal—Bronze; *Event*—Mixed Team 10 m Air Pistol (with Manu Bhaker).
3. Swapnil Kusale; Medal—Bronze; *Event*—50 m rifle 3 position.
4. Neeraj Chopra, Medal—Silver; *Event*—Men's Javelin Throw.
5. Aman Sehrawat; Medal—Bronze; *Event*—Men's Free Style 57 kg wrestling.

33rd Paris Olympics 2024; Top 10 Medal Winner Countries

Position	Country	Gold	Silver	Bronze	Total Medals
1	United States (USA)	40	44	42	126
2	China (CHN)	40	27	24	91
3	Japan (JPN)	20	12	13	45
4	Australia (USA)	18	19	16	53
5	France (FRA)	16	26	22	64
6	Netherlands (NED)	15	7	12	34
7	United Kingdom (GBR)	14	22	29	65
8	South Korea (KOR)	13	9	10	32
9	Itlay (ITA)	12	13	15	40
10	Germany (GER)	12	13	8	33
71	**India**	***00***	***01***	**05**	**06**

34th Olympics 2028 proposed—Los Angeles (U.S.A.)

35th Olympics 2032 proposed—Brisbane (Australia)

Important Sport Results

FOOTBALL

UEFA Nations League 2025 (4–8 June, 2025)—Winner—Portugal, Runner up—Spain

Indian Super League (ISL 2024-25)—Winner—Mohan Bagan

Swami Vivekanand Men's U-20 National Football Championship 2025—Winner—Delhi

38th National Games 2025 (Men's Football)—Winner—Kerala

SAFF (U-19) Football (Men's 2025)—Winner—India

UEFA Euro Cup (June-July 2024)—Spain.

Copa del Rey (2024-25)—Barcelona.

UEFA Champions League (2024)—Winner—Real Madrid.

English Premier League (May 2024)—Manchester City.

Africa Cup of Nations 2023 (Feb. 2024, Ivory Cost)—Ivory Cost beat Nigeria.

UEFA Super Cup (August 2024, Poland)—Real Madrid.

FIFA Women's Under-17 World Cup 2022 (Nov. 2024)—North Korea defeated Spain.

Santosh Trophy 2024-25 (Dec. 2024)—Winner—West Bengal.

Durand Cup (2024)—North East United

FIFA World Cup Football 2022 (Nov.-Dec. 2022)—Argentina defeated France in the final.

FIFA Women's World Cup Football 2023 (August 2023, Australia and New Zealand)—Spain defeated England in the final.

CHESS

87th Tata Steel Masters 2025—R. Praggnanandhaa

Prague Chess Festival Masters 2025—Aravindh Chithambaram

World Junior Chess Championships 2025—Men's Title—Pranav, Women's Title—Anna Shukhnan

World Chess Championship 2024—Gukesh D. (India)

10th Leon Masters Chess 2024—Viswanathan Anand wins.

FIDE Chess World Cup 2023 (August 2023, Baku)—Magnus Carlsen

50th National Women Chess Championship (Oct. 2024)—Nandhidhaa P.V..

61st National Senior Chess Championship (August 2024)—Kartik Venkatraman.

Commonwealth Chess Championship-2023-34 (Malacca, Malaysia)—Men's Winner : Mitrabha Guha, Women's Winner : Gong Qianyun (Singapore).

Women's World Chess Championship 2024 (Dec. 2024)—Koneru Humpy

FIDE U-20 Girls World Junior Chess Championship 2025—Men's Winner : Pranav (India), Women's Winner : Anna Shukhman (Russia).

45th Chess Olympiad (2024)—India (Women's and Open categories—Gold).

GOLF

The Open Championship (July 2024, Scotland)—Xander Schauffele.

Women's British Open 2024 (August 2024)—Lydia Ko (New Zealand)

Augusta Masters (April 2025)—Rory Mellory

U.S. Women's Open Golf Championship 2025 (June 2025)—Maja Stork (Sweden)

US Open Golf (June 2025)—J.J. Spaun

PGA Championship 2025 (May 2025)—Scottie Scheffler

CRICKET

ICC Women's Under-19 T20 World Cup (Jan. 2025)—India beat South Africa.

Women's Asia Cup (2024)—Sri Lanka.

Syed Mushtaq Ali Trophy (2024-25)—Mumbai beat Madhya Pradesh.

Asia Cup Cricket (Sep. 2023)—India beat Sri Lanka.

ICC Men's T-20 World Cup (June 2024)—India defeated South Africa.

Border-Gavaskar Trophy (2024-25)—Austrial beat India.

ICC Women's Under-19 T-20 Cricket World Cup 2025 (Feb. 2025)—Winner : India, Runner up : South Africa.

ICC Men's Under-19 Cricket World Cup (2024)—Australia wins.

ICC World Cup Cricket 2023 (Oct.-Nov. 2023, India)—Australia defeated India.

18th IPL Cricket Tournament (June 2025)—Royal Challengers Bengaluru defeated Punjab Kings.

ICC World Test Championship (June 2023)—Australia defeated India.

13th ICC Women's Cricket World Cup (2023) (February 2023)—Australia beat South Africa.

ICC Women's T-20 World Cup (2024, UAE)—Winner : New Zealand, Runner-up : South Africa.

Deodhar Trophy (2023-24)—South Zone.

Duleep Trophy (2024-25)—India A winner.

Vijay Hazare Trophy (2024-25)—Karnataka defeated Vidarbha.

Irani Trophy 2024-25—Winner : Mumbai, Runner-up : Rest of India.

Ranji Trophy (2024-25)—Winner : Vidarbha, Runner-up : Kerala.

TENNIS

French Open (2025)—*Men's Singles* : Carlos Alcaraz (Spain), *Women's Singles* : Coco Gauff (USA)

Laver Cup (2024)—Europe.

Qutar Open (2025)—Andrey Rublev.

ATP Monte Carlo Masters Cup (2025)—Carlos Alcaraz.

BNP Paribas Open (March 2025)—Men's Singles : Jack Drafer (UK), *Women's Singles* : Mirra Andreeva (Russia).

Australian Open Men's Singles (2025)—Jannik Sinner (Italy).

Australia Open Women's Singles (2025)—Medison Keys (USA).

Wimbledon Tennis (July 2024)—*Men's Singles* : Carlos Alcaraj (Spain), *Women's Singles* : Barbora Krejcikova (Czech Republic).

U.S. Open Tennis (2024)—*Men's Singles* : Yannick Sinner; *Women's Singles* : Aryna Sabalenka.

Davis Cup 2024 (Nov. 2024)—Italy defeated Netherland in final.

Hopman Cup (2023)—Croatia.

Madrid Open (2025)—*Men's Singles* : Casfer Ruud (Norway), *Women's Singles* : Aryna Sabalenka (Belarus).

Italian Open (2024)—*Men's Singles* : Alexander Zverev, *Women's Singles* : Iga Swiatek.

HOCKEY

15th Hockey India Senior Women's National Championship 2025—*Winner—Jharkhand, Runner-up—Haryana*

15th Hockey Senior Men National Championship—Winner—Punjab, Runner-up—Madhya Pradesh

Women's Hockey 5s World Cup 2024—Netherlands wins.

Hockey Asia Cup (Women) 2024, (Nov. 2024, India)—India defeated China.

Sultan of Johar Cup 2024 (Oct. 2024, Malaysia)–Great Britain defeated Australia.

Beighton Cup (2024)—Indian Navy.

2024 Men's Hockey Asia Cup (Dec. 2024, Muscut)—India defeated Pakistan.

Men's Hockey 5s World Cup (Jan. 2024)—Netherlands wins.

Sultan Azlan Shah Cup (2024)—Japan wins.

BADMINTON

BWF Indian Open (2025)—*Men's Singles* : Viktor Axelsen (Denmark), *Women's Singles* : An Se-Young (South Korea).

French Open (2024)—*Men's Singles* : Jonatan Christie (Indonesia), *Women's Singles* : Chen Yu Fei (China).

BWF Malaysia Open (2025)—*Men's Singles* : Shi Yuqi (China); *Women's Singles* : An Se Young (South Korea).

Sudirman Cup 2025 (May 2025)—China.

Thomas Cup 2024 (May 2024)—China.

Indonesia Open 2024—*Men's Singles* : Shi Yuqi, *Women's Singles* : Chen YuFei.

World Badminton Championship 2023 (August 2023)—*Men's Singles* : Kunpavut Vitidsam (Thailand), *Women's Singles* : An Se-Young (South Korea).

BWF Singapore Open 2024—*Men's Singles* : Shi Yuqi, *Women's Singles* : An Se-young.

Indonesia Masters-2025—*Women's* : Ratchanok Intanon (Thailand); *Men's Singles* : Kunpavut Vitidsarn (Thailand).

All-England Open Badminton Championship (March 2025)—*Men's Singles* : Shi Yuqi (China), *Women's Singles* : An Se-Young (South Korea).

Uber Cup 2024 (May 2024)—China.

Korea Open (Sept. 2024)—*Men's Singles* : Lu Guangzu (China) *Women's Singles* : Kim Ga-eun (South Korea)

Denmark Open (Oct. 2024)—*Men's Singles* : Anders Antonsen (Denmark), *Women's Singles* : Warg Zhiyi

Syed Modi International Badminton Championship 2024 (Dec. 2024, Lucknow)—*Men's Singles* : Lakshya Sen (India), Women's Singles : P.V. Sindhu (India)

Malaysia Masters (2024)—*Men's Singles* : Viktor Axelsen; *Women's Singles* : Wang ZhiYi.

BWF Australian Open (2024)—*Men's Singles* : Lee Zii Jia; *Women's Singles* : Aya Ohori.

SOME IMPORTANT NATIONAL AWARDS

Republic Day Honours

Indian Government gives honour to the illustrious men in various fields on 26th January each year. Main honours are—Bharat Ratna, Padma Vibhushan, Padma Bhushan and Padma Shri.

In January 2025, the President has approved conferment of 139 Padma Awards including 1 duo cases (in a duo case, the Award is counted as one) as per list below. The list comprises 7 Padma Vibhushan 19, Padma Bhushan and 113 Padma Shri Awards. 23 of the awardees are women and the list also includes 10 persons from the category of Foreigners/NRI/PIO/OCI and 13 Posthumous awardees.

Padma Vibhushan (7)

S.N.	Name	Field	State/Country
1.	Shri Duvvur Nageshwar Reddy	Medicine	Telangana
2.	Justice (Retd.) Shri Jagdish Singh Khehar	Public Affairs	Chandigarh
3.	Smt. Kumudini Rajnikant Lakhia	Art	Gujarat
4.	Shri Lakshminaryana Subramaniam	Art	Karnataka
5.	Shri M.T. Vasudevan Nair (Posthumous)	Literature and Education	Kerala
6.	Shri Osamu Suzuki (Posthumous)	Trade and Industry	Japan
7.	Smt. Sharda Sinha (Posthumous)	Art	Bihar

Padma Bhushan (19)

1.	Shri A. Surya Prakash	Literature and Education-Journalism	Karnataka
2.	Shri Anant Nag	Art	Karnataka
3.	Shri Bibek Debroy (Posthumous)	Literature and Education	NCT Delhi
4.	Shri Jatin Goswami	Art	Assam
5.	Shri Jose Chacko Periappuram	Medicine	Kerala
6.	Shri Kailash Nath Dikshit	Others-Archaeology	NCT Delhi
7.	Shri Joshi Manohar (Posthumous)	Public Affairs	Maharashtra
8.	Shri Nalli Kuppuswami Chetti	Trade and Industry	Tamil Nadu
9.	Shri Nandamuri Balakrishna	Art	Andhra Pradesh
10.	Shri P. R. Sreejesh	Sports	Kerala
11.	Shri Pankaj Patel	Trade and Industry	Gujarat
12.	Shri Pankaj Udhas (Posthumous)	Art	Maharashtra
13.	Shri Rambahadur Rai	Literature and Education-Journalism	Uttar Pradesh
14.	Sadhvi Ritambhara	Social Work	Uttar Pradesh
15.	Shri S. Ajith Kumar	Art	Tamil Nadu
16.	Shri Shekhar Kapur	Art	Maharashtra
17.	Ms. Shobana Chandrakumar	Art	Tamil Nadu
18.	Shri Sushil Kumar Modi (Posthumous)	Public Affaris	Bihar
19.	Shri Vinod Dham	Science and Engineering	United States of America

Bharat Ratna—Bharat Ratna is the Nation's highest honour, which is awarded for exceptional and distinguished services of a high order in any field, *i.e.*, art, literature, science and public service.

The following are the recipients of the Bharat Ratna :

Recipients of Bharat Ratna

1.	Dr. S. Radhakrishnan	1954
2.	C. Rajagopalachari	1954
3.	C. V. Raman	1954
4.	Dr. Bhagwan Das	1955
5.	Dr. M. Visveswaraiya	1955
6.	Jawahar Lal Nehru	1955
7.	Govind Ballabh Pant	1957
8.	Dr. D. K. Karve	1958
9.	Dr. B. C. Roy	1961
10.	Purusottam Das Tondon	1961
11.	Dr. Rajendra Prasad	1962
12.	Dr. Zakir Hussain	1963
13.	Dr. P.V. Kane	1963
14.	Lal Bahadur Shastri*	1966
15.	Smt. Indira Gandhi	1971
16.	V. V. Giri	1975
17.	K. Kamraj*	1976
18.	Mother Teresa	1980
19.	Acharya Vinoba Bhave*	1983
20.	Khan Abdul Gaffar Khan	1987
21.	M. G. Ramchandran*	1988
22.	Dr. B. R. Ambedkar*	1990
23.	Nelson Mandela	1990
24.	Morarji Desai	1991
25.	Rajiv Gandhi*	1991
26.	Sardar V. B. Patel*	1991
27.	M. Abul Kalam Azad*	1992
28.	J.R.D. Tata	1992
29.	Satyajit Ray	1992
30.	Guljari Lal Nanda	1997
31.	Aruna Asaf Ali*	1997
32.	Dr. A.P.J. Abdul Kalam	1997
33.	M.S. Subbalaxami	1998
34.	C. S. Subramaniam	1998
35.	Jai Prakash Narain*	1998
36.	Prof. Amartya Sen	1999
37.	Pt. Ravi Shankar	1999
38.	Gopinath Bordoloi	1999
39.	Lata Mangeshkar	2001
40.	Bismillah Khan	2001
41.	Pt. Bhimsen Joshi	2008
42.	Sachin Tendulkar	2014
43.	C.N.R. Rao	2014
44.	A. B. Vajpaiyee	2015
45.	Madan Mohan Malviya*	2015
46.	Pranab Mukherjee	2019
47.	Nanajee Deshmukh	2019
48.	Bhupen Hazarika	2019
49.	Lal Krishna Advani	2024
50.	Karpoori Thakur*	2024
51.	M.S. Swaminathan*	2024
52.	P.V. Narasimha Rao*	2024
53.	Chaudhary Charan Singh*	2024

*Posthumously

Note—Lal Bahadur Shastri was the first person to be honoured with Bharat Ratna posthumously and Indira Gandhi was the first women recipient of Bharat Ratna.

Dada Sahib Phalke Award—Instituted in 1970 this award is given by the Ministry of Information & Broadcasting to Indian Film Industry. The recipients are :

1.	Mrs. Devika Rani Roerich	1969
2.	B. N. Sirkar	1970
3.	Prithvi Raj Kapoor	1971
4.	Pankaj Mallick	1972
5.	Mrs. Ruby Myers	1973
6.	B. N. Reddy	1974
7.	Dhiren Ganguly	1975
8.	Mrs. Kanan Devi	1976
9.	Nitin Bose	1977
10.	R. C. Boral	1978
11.	Sohrab Modi	1979
12.	P. Jai Raj	1980
13.	Naushad Ali	1981
14.	L. V. Prasad	1982
15.	Mrs. Durga Khote	1983
16.	Satyajit Ray	1984
17.	V. Shantaram	1985
18.	V. Nagi Reddy	1986
19.	Raj Kapoor	1987
20.	Ashok Kumar	1988
21.	Lata Mangeshkar	1989
22.	A. Nageshwar Rao	1990
23.	Bhalji Pendharkar	1991
24.	Bhupen Hazarika	1992
25.	Majrooh Sultanpuri	1993
26.	Dilip Kumar	1994
27.	Dr. Raj Kumar	1995
28.	Shivaji Ganeshan	1996
29.	Kavi Pradeep	1997
30.	B. R. Chopra	1998
31.	Hrishikesh Mukherjee	1999
32.	Asha Bhonsle	2000

33.	Yash Chopra	2001
34.	Devanand	2002
35.	Mrinal Sen	2003
36.	Adoor Gopalkrishnan	2004
37.	Shyam Bengal	2005
38.	Tapan Sinha	2006
39.	Manna Dey	2007
40.	V. K. Murthy	2008
41.	D. Ramanaidu	2009
42.	K. Balachander	2010
43.	Saumitra Chatterjee	2011
44.	Pran	2012
45.	Sampooran Singh Kalra (Gulzar)	2013
46.	Shashi Kapoor	2014
47.	Manoj Kumar	2015
48.	K. Vishwanath	2016
49.	Vinod Khanna	2017
50.	Amitabh Bachhan	2018
51.	Rajnikanth	2019
52.	Asha Parekh	2020
53.	Waheeda Rehman	2021
54.	Mithun Chakraborty	2022

Gallantry Awards

1. Param Vir Chakra—The highest award for bravery for daring or pre-eminent act or valour or self-sacrifice in the presence of the enemy, whether on land, at sea or in air. The recipients of the highest gallantry award for 1999 were Capt. Vikram Batra (Posthumous), Lt. Manoj Kumar Pandey (Posthumous), Grenadier Yogender Singh Yadav and Rifleman Sanjay Kumar.

2. Maha Vir Chakra—It is the second highest decoration and is awarded for acts of conspicuous gallantry in the presence of the enemy, whether on land, at sea or in air. Colonel Santosh Babu (Bihar Regiment) 2021.

3. Vir Chakra—It is the third in order of awards given for acts of gallantry in the presence of the enemy, whether on land, at sea or in air.

From 1988 the Union Govt. has started awarding two more medals in the Category of Gallantry Awards—

4. Uttam Yudh Sewa Padak

5. Yudh Sewa Padak

6. Ashok Chakra—This medal is awarded for an act of most conspicuous bravery or some daring or pre-eminent act of valour or self-sacrifice on land, at sea or in air but not in the presence of the enemy. It has three categories : I, II and III. II category medal is called Kirti Chakra and III category medal Shaurya Chakra.

Other National Awards

Saraswati Samman—Field : For outstanding contribution to Literature in any language given in 8th Schedule.

Institution—K.K. Birla Foundation.

Amount—₹ 10 lakh.

1st Award—Harivansh Rai Bachchan (1991).

2012—Sugatha Kumari.

2013—Govind Mishra (Hindi).

2014—Veerappa Moily (Kannada)

2015—Padma Sachdeva (Dogri)

2016—*Mahabaleshwar Sail (Konkani)*

2017—Sitanshu Yashaschandra

2018—K. Siva Reddy

2019—Vasdev Mohi
2020—Sharan Kumar Limbale
2021—Ramdarash Mishra
2022—Shivshankari.
2023—Prabha Verma.
2024—Sadhu Bhadreshdas (Book–'Swaminarayan Siddhanta Shudha').

National Sports Awards 2024

Major Dhyan Chand Khel Ratna Award (2024)—The Major Dhyan Chand Khel Ratna Award is the highest honor given to an athlete for their exceptional performance over four years. This award commemorates Major Dhyan Chand, India's hockey legend. Below is the list of recipients for 2024 :

S.No.	Name of the Sportsperson	Discipline
1.	Shri Gukesh D.	Chess
2.	Shri Harmanpreet Singh	Hockey
3.	Shri Praveen Kumar	Para-Athletics
4.	Ms. Manu Bhaker	Shooting

1. Arjuna Awards 2024 for Outstanding Performance in Sports and Games—The **Arjuna Awards** recognize exceptional athletes for their outstanding achievements and contributions to Indian sports. Below is the list of recipients for the **Arjuna Awards 2024**, honoring excellence across various disciplines. :

Arjuna Awards 2024 Recipients

S.No.	Name of the Sportsperson	Discipline
1.	Ms. Jyothi Yarraji	Athletics
2.	Ms. Annu Rani	Athletics
3.	Ms. Nitu	Boxing
4.	Ms. Saweety	Boxing
5.	Ms. Vantika Agrawal	Chess
6.	Ms. Salima Tete	Hockey
7.	Shri Abhishek	Hockey
8.	Shri Sanjay	Hockey
9.	Shri Jarmanpreet Singh	Hockey
10.	Shri Sukhjeet Singh	Hockey
11.	Shri Rakesh Kumar	Para-Archery
12.	Ms. Preeti Pal	Para-Athletics
13.	Ms. Jeevanji Deepthi	Para-Athletics
14.	Shri Ajeet Singh	Para-Athletics
15.	Shri Sachin Sarjerao Khilari	Para-Athletics
16.	Shri Dharambir	Para-Athletics

17.	Shri Pranav Soorma	Para-Athletics
18.	Shri H. Hokato Sema	Para-Athletics
19.	Ms. Simran	Para-Athletics
20.	Shri Navdeep	Para-Athletics
21.	Shri Nitesh Kumar	Para-Badminton
22.	Ms. Thulasimathi Murugesan	Para-Badminton
23.	Ms. Nithya Sre Sumathy Sivan	Para-Badminton
24.	Ms. Manisha Ramadass	Para-Badminton
25.	Shri Kapil Parmar	Para-Judo
26.	Ms. Mona Agarwal	Para-Shooting
27.	Ms. Rubina Francis	Para-Shooting
28.	Shri Swapnil Suresh Kusale	Shooting
29.	Shri Sarabjot Singh	Shooting
30.	Shri Abhay Singh	Squash
31.	Shri Sajan Prakash	Swimming
32.	Shri Aman	Wrestling

2. Arjuna Awards 2024 (Lifetime Achievement)—The **Lifetime Achievement Arjuna Awards** are presented to individuals for their remarkable contributions and dedication to sports throughout their careers.

S.No.	Name of the Sportsperson	Discipline
1.	Shri Sucha Singh	Athletics
2.	Shri Murlikant Rajaram Petkar	Para-Swimming

Dronacharya Award (2024)—The Dronacharya Award is presented to coaches who have demonstrated exceptional skill in nurturing talent and guiding athletes to achieve excellence.

Dronacharya Award 2024 for Outstanding Coaches in Sports and Games—The Dronacharya Award honours exceptional coaches who have consistently guided athletes to achieve excellence in sports. The awards are presented in two categories. Regular and Lifetime. Below are the details of the recipients for 2024 :

Regular Category

S.No.	Name of the Coach	Discipline
1.	Shri Subhash Rana	Para-Shooting
2.	Ms. Deepali Deshpande	Shooting
3.	Shri Sandeep Sangwan	Hockey

Lifetime Category

S.No.	Name of the Coach	Discipline
1.	Shri S. Muralidharan	Badminton
2.	Shri Armando Agnelo Colaco	Football

Maulana Abul Kalam Azad Trophy (2024)—The Maulana Abul Kalam Azad Trophy is awarded to universities that excel in promoting sports activities. The Maulana Abul Kalam Azad (MAKA) Trophy is awarded annually to the university excelling in sports and inter-university tournaments across India. This prestigious honor recognizes the efforts of universities in fostering sportsmanship, talent and competitive spirit among students. Below is the list of winners for the **Maka Trophy 2024 :**

MAKA Trophy 2024 Winners

S.No.	Name of University	Position
1.	Chandigarh University	Overall Winner University
2.	Lovely Professional University (PB)	1st Runner-Up University
3.	Guru Nanak Dev University, Amritsar	2nd Runner-Up University

Rashtriya Khel Protsahan Puraskar 2024—The Rashtriya Khel Protsahan Puraskar honors individuals and organizations that contribute to the development and promotion of sports.

The Rashtriya Khel Protsahan Puraskar is awarded to organizations and entities that have made significant contributions to the promotion and development of sports in India. This award recognizes their efforts in encouraging sports culture and nurturing talent.

Recipient of Rashtriya Khel Protsahan Puraskar 2024

S.No.	Name of the Entity
1.	Physical Education Foundation of India

Recipients of Jnanpith Award

1. G. Shankar Kurup 1965
2. T. S. Bandopadhyaya 1966
3. Uma Shankar Joshi 1967
4. Sumitra Nandan Pant 1968
5. R. S. Firaq Gorakhpuri 1969
6. Vishwanath Satyanarayan 1970
7. Prishnu Roy 1971
8. Ram Dhari Singh Dinkar 1972
9. Dr. D. R. Bendre and Gopinath Mohanty 1973
10. V. S. Khandekar 1974
11. P.V. Akilandam 1975
12. Mrs. Asha Purna Devi 1976
13. K. Shiv Ram Karanth 1977
14. H. S. Vatsayan 'Ageya' 1978
15. B. K. Bhattacharya 1979
16. S. K. Pottekat 1980
17. Mrs. Amrita Pritam 1981
18. Mrs. Mahadevi Verma 1982
19. M. V. Iyangar 1983
20. T. S. Pillai 1984
21. Panna Lal Patel 1985
22. Sachidanand Routroy 1986
23. V. V. Shirvadkar 1987
24. C. Narayana Reddy 1988
25. Qurtul-N-Haider 1989
26. Vinayak Krishan Gokak 1990
27. Subhash Mukhopadhyay 1991
28. Naresh Mehta 1992
29. Dr. Sitakant Mahapatra 1993
30. U. R. Anantha Murthy 1994
31. M. T. Vasudevan Nair 1995
32. Smt. Mahasweta Devi 1996
33. Ali Sardar Jafari 1997
34. Girish Karnad 1998
35. Nirmal Verma and Gurdayal Singh 1999

36.	Indira Goswami	2000	49.	Ravuri Bharadwaja	2012
37.	Rajendra Keshav Lal Shah	2001	50.	Kedarnath Singh	2013
38.	D. Jayakanthan	2002	51.	Bhalchandra Nemade	2014
39.	Vinda Karandikar	2003	52.	Raghuveer Chaudhary	2015
40.	Rahman Rahi	2004	53.	Shankha Ghosh	2016
41.	Kunwar Narayan	2005	54.	Krishna Sobati	2017
42.	Ravindra Kelkar	2006	55.	Amitav Ghose	2018
43.	Satya Vrat Shastri	2006	56.	Akkitham Achuthan Namboothiri	2019
44.	ONV Kurup	2007	57.	Nilamani Phookan (Assamese)	2021
45.	Ablag Khan Shaharyar	2008	58.	Damodar Mauzo (Konkani)	2022
46.	Shrilal Shukla	2009	59.	Gulzar and Jagadguru Rambhadracharya	2023
47.	Chandrashekhar Kambar	2010			
48.	Dr. Pratibha Rai	2011			

70th National Film Awards : Major Winners

(Announced in August 2024)

- **Best Feature Film :** Aattam (Malayalam movie)
- **Best Actor :** Rishab Shetty, Kantara
- **Best Actress :** Nithya Menen in Tiruchitrabalam, and Manasi Parekh in Kutch Express
- **Best Director :** Sooraj Barjatya for Uunchai
- **Best Supporting Actress :** Neena Gupta for Uunchai
- **Best Supporting Actor :** Pawan Malhotra, Fouja
- **Best Feature Film Providing Wholesome Entertainment :** Kantara (Kannada movie)
- **Best Debut Film of a Director :** Fouja directed by Pramod Kumar
- **Best Action Direction :** KGF : Chapter 2
- **Best Choreography :** Tiruchitrabalam
- **Best Lyrics :** Fouja
- **Best Music Director :** Pritam (Songs), A.R. Rahman (Background Score)
- **Best Makeup :** Aparajito
- **Best Costumes :** Kutch Express
- **Best Production Design :** Aparajito
- **Best Editing :** Aattam
- **Best Sound Design :** Ponniyin Selvan – Part 1
- **Best Screenplay :** Aattam
- **Best Dialogues :** Gulmohar
- **Best Cinematography :** Ponniyin Selvan – Part 1
- **Best Female Playback :** Saudi Velakka CC.225/2009, Bombay Jayashri
- **Best Male Playback :** Brahmastra, Arijit Singh
- **Best Child Artist :** Sreepath in Mallikappuram
- **Best Film in AVGC :** Brahmastra – Part 1
- **Best Non-Feature Film Promoting Social and Environmental Values :** Kutch Express (Gujarati movie)

Non-Feature Categories

- **Best Non-Feature Film :** Ayena
- **Best Script :** Mono No Aware
- **Best Music Director :** Fursat
- **Best Short Film :** Xunyota
- **Best Direction :** From the Shadow

81th Golden Globe Awards (2025)

- **Best Film (Drama) :** Oppenheimer
- **Best Actress (Drama) :** Lily Gladstone, Killers of the Flower Moon
- **Best Film (Musical or Comedy) :** Poor Things
- **Best Actor (Musical Comedy) :** Paul Giamatti, The Holdovers
- **Best TV Series (Drama) :** Succeession
- **Best Actress in a TV Series (Drama) :** Sarah Snook, Succession
- **Best TV Series (Musical or Comedy) :** The Bear
- **Best Limited Series, Anthology Series or TV Movie :** Beef
- **Cinematic and Box Office Achievement :** Barbie
- **Best Original Song :** What Was I Made For ? by Billie Eillish and Finneas (Barbie)
- **Best Original Score :** Ludwing Goransson, Oppenheimer
- **Best Actor (Drama) :** Cillian Murphy, Oppenheimer
- **Best Actress (Musical or Comedy) :** Emma Stone, Poor Things
- **Best Director :** Christopher Nolan, Oppenheimer
- **Best Animated Film :** The Boy and the Heron
- **Best Actress in a TV Series (Drama) :** Kieran Culkin, Succession
- **Best Actress in a TV Series (Musical or Comedy) :** Ayo Edebriri, The Bear
- **Best Non-English Language Film :** Anatomy of a Fall
- **Best Performance in Stand-up Comedy on TV :** Ricky Gervais, Ricky, Gervais Armageddon
- **Best Actor in a TV Series (Musical or Comedy) :** Jeremy Allen White, The Bear
- **Best Screenplay :** Justine Triet and Arthur Harari, Anatomy of a Fall
- **Best Supporting Actor in a TV Series :** Mathew Macfadyen, Succession
- **Best Supporting Actress in a TV Series :** Elizabeth Debicki, The Crown
- **Best Actor in a Limited Serie, Anthology Series or TV Movie :** Steven Yeun, Beef
- **Best Actress in a Limited Series, Anthology Series or TV Movie :** Ali Wong, Beef
- **Best Supporting Actor :** Brobert Downey Jr, Oppenheimer.
- **Best Supporting Actress :** De'Vine Joy Randolph, The Holdovers

Laureus World Sports Awards (2024)

- **Laureus World Sportsman of the Year Award :** Novak Djokovic.
- **Laureus World Sportswoman of the Year Award :** Aitana Bonmati.
- **Laureus World Team of the Year Award :** Spain Women's Football Team.
- **Laureus World Breakthrough of the Year Award :** Jude Bellingham.
- **Laureus World Comeback of the Year Award :** Simone Biles.
- **Laureus Sport for Good Award :** Foundation Rafa Nadal.
- **Laureus World Sportsperson of the Year with a Disability Award :** Diede de Groot.
- **Laureus World Action Sportsperson of the Year Award :** Arisa Trew.

Ramon Magsaysay Award Winners (2024)

Awardee Name	Country	Contribution
Karma Phuntsho	Bhutan	Honoured for bridging Bhutan's rick heritage with modern challenges, inspiring young Bhutanese to embrace their past while confidently moving forward.
Miyazaki Hayao	Japan	Honoured for using animation to illustrate the human condition, especially inspiring children as torchbearers of imagination.
Rural Doctors Movement	Thailand	Improving public health and empowering rural citizens, ensuring no one is left behind in the country's progress.
Nguyen Thi Ngoc Phuong	Vietnam	Honoured for her research on Agent Orange's/Dioxin's impact and her dedication to supporting its victims, highlighting the long-term consequences of war.
Farwiza Farhan	Indonesia	Environmentalist and Social Justice Advocate.

Jamna Lal Bajaj Awards (2024)

Constructive Work—Girija Nandan (Jharkhand), **Science and Technology for Rural Development**—Rashmi Bharti (Uttarakhand) **Women & Child Welfare**—Dr. Tulsi Munda (Odisha), **International Award for Promoting Gandhian Values Outside India**—Reverend Erik Kunedisa (Democratic Republic of Cango) .

Other Awards

Miss World 2025—Opal Suchata Chuangsri (Thailand)

International Booker Prize 2025—Banu Mushtaq (India) (Book—Heart Lamp)

Time's Person of the Year (2024)—Donald Trump (USA).

Aryabhatta Award 2025—Dr. G. Vijay Kumar

Miss Universe 2024—Alejandra Marisa Rodriguez (Argentina).

International Booker Prize 2024—Jenny Erpenbeck (Kaiors-Novel).

Booker Prize (2024)—Samantha Harvey (Orbital).

Sydney Peace Prize 2025—Navi Pillay

24th Lal Bahadur Shastri Award for Excellence (2024)—Smt. Rajashree Birla.

Sakharov Prize (2024)—Maria Corina Machado (Venezuela)

Mother Teresa Memorial Award (2024)—Late. Ratan Tata.

Indira Gandhi Prize for Peace, Disarmament and Development for 2024—Michelle Bachlet (Former President of Chile).

Mahatma Gandhi Peace Prize (2023)—Gita Press, Gorakhpur.

M.P. Govt.'s Kishore Kumar Samman (2023)—Raj Kumar Hirani.

Guillermo Cano World Press Freedom Prize (2024)—Palestinian Journalists.

C. K. Nayudu Award for Lifetime Achievement (2025)—Sachin Tendulkar.

Seol Peace Prize (2025)—Direct Relief.

Forbes' Most Powerful Woman (2024)—Ursula von der Leyen.

34rd Vyas Puraskar (2024)—Suryabala

Abel Prize (2025)—*Masaki Kashiware.*

FIH Best Player (Men) (2024)—Harman Preet Singh (India).

FIH Best Player (Women) (2024)—Yibbi Jansen (Netherland).

Pritzker Architecture Prize (2025)—Liu Jiakun (China)
FIFA Best Player (Men) (2024)—Lionel Messi (Argentina).
FIFA Woman Player of World (2024)—Aitana Bonmati.
G. D. Birla Award for Scientific Research (2025)—Prof. Narayan Pradhan and Prof. Neelesh B. Mehta
Sastra Ramanujan Prize (2024)—Alexander Dunn
Lokmanya Tilak National Award (2024)—Sudha Murty.
World Food Prize (2025)—Dr. Mariangela Hungria
Fukuoka Prize (2024)—Sunil Amrith Manabe Daito and Kimsooja.
Vaclav Havel Prize (2024)—Maria Carina Machado (Venezuela).
Chameli Devi Jain Award (2025)—Jatinder Kaur Tur.
Lata Deenanath Mangeshkar Award (2025)—Kumar Mangalam Birla.
Templeton Prize (2025)—Bartholomew-I (Turkey).

Nobel Prizes For 2024

Field	Nobel Prize Winners	Awarded For
Physiology/Medicine	Victor Ambros (USA) Gary Ruvkun (USA)	Discovery of micro RNAs
Physics	John J. Hopfield (USA) Geoffrey E. Hinton (British-Canadian)	Use of statistical physics concepts in the development of artificial neural networks
Chemistry	David Baker (USA) Demis Hassabis (British) and John M. Jumper (USA)	To David Baker 'for computational protein design'. Demis Hassabis and John M. Jumper 'for protein structure prediction'.
Literature	Han Kang (South Korean writer)	For her intense poetic prose that confronts historical traumas and exposes the fragility of human life.
Peace	Nihon Hidankyo (Japanese organisation)	For its efforts to achieve a world free of nuclear weapons and for demonstrating through witness testimony that nuclear weapons must never be used again
Economics	Daron Acemoglu, Simon Johnson and James A. Robinson (USA)	For studies of how institutions are formed and affect prosperity

Rashtriya Vigyan Puraskar 2024—The Rashtriya Vigyan Puraskar (RVP) is a prestigious set of awards that recognize and encourage significant achievements by scientists, technologists and innovators of Indian origin, including Persons of Indian Origin (PIO), whether working in India or abroad. These awards **honour individuals who have made distinguished** contributions through impactful research, innovation or discovery that benefits Indian communities or society. The RVP is being **introduced for the first**

time in 2024. It was established to replace the existing science awards, including the **Shanti Swarup Bhatnagar Prize,** to provide a more inclusive and updated recognition system. The new awards allow for a more comprehensive acknowledgement of achievements. These awards shall be announced on **11th May (National Technology Day) ever year.** The Award Ceremony for all categories of awards will be held on **National Space Day. RVP is awarded in various categories** such as Physical Sciences, Chemical Sciences, Biological Sciences, Mathematical Sciences, Earth & Atmospheric Sciences and Engineering Sciences.

Categories of the Awards :

(1) Vigyan Ratna, (2) Vigyan Shri, (3) Vigyan Yuva, (4) Vigyan Team

Award Category	Recipient(s)	Field
Vigyan Ratna Puraskar	Dr. Govindarajan Padmanabhan	Biochemistry
Vigyan Shri	Dr. Annapurini Subramanian	Astrophysics
	Dr. Anandharamakrishanan C	Agriculture Sciences
	Dr. Avesh Kumar Tyagi	Atomic Energy
	Prof. Umesh Varshney, Prof. Jayant Bhalchandra Udgaonkar	Biological Sciences
	Prof. Syed Wajih Ahmad Naqvi	Earth Sciences
	Prof. Bhim Singh	Engineering Sciences
	Prof. Adimurthi Adi, Prof. Rahul Mukherjee	Mathematics and Computer Science
	Prof. Dr. Sanjay Behari	Medicine
	Prof. Lakshmanan Muthusamy, Prof. Naba Kumar Mondal	Physics
	Prof. Rohit Srivastava	Technology and Innovation
Vigyan Yuva	Krishna Murthy SL, Swarup Kumar Parida	Agricultural Science
	Radhakrishan Mahalakshmi, Prof. Aravind Penmatsa	Biological Sciences
	Vivek Polshettiwar, Vishal Rai	Chemistry
	Roxy Mathew Koll	Earth Sciences
	Abhilash, Radha Krishna Ganti	Engineering Sciences
	Purabi Saikia, Bappi Paul	Environmental Science
	Mahesh Ramesh Kakde	Mathematics and Computer Science
	Jitendra Kumar Sahu, Pragya Dhruv Yadav	Medicine
	Urbasi Sinha	Physics
	Digendranath Swain, Prashant Kumar	Space Science and Technology
	Prabhu Rajagopal	Technology and Innovation
Vigyan Team	Team Chandrayaan-3	Space Science

HISTORY

Important Dates of World History

B. C.

776 First Olympic Games in Greece .

A.D.

29 Crucifixion of Jesus Christ

78 Start of Saka Era

570 Birth of Prophet Mohammed at Mecca

1453 Renaissance in Europe

1492 Columbus discovered America

1588 Defeat of Spanish Armada

1649 King Charles I beheaded-beginning of Commonwealth in England.

1688 Glorious Revolution in England.

1776 American Colonies declared independent (4th July)

1789 French Revolution.

1805 Battle of Trafalgar

1815 Battle of Waterloo-Napoleon defeated, exiled to St. Helena.

1869 Suez Canal opened for traffic, Gandhi was born.

1891 Birth of Bhim Rao Ambedkar.

1904 Russian-Japanese War.

1914-1918 World War I (July 28, 1914-Nov. 11, 1918)

1917 Russian Bolshevik Revolution and the assassination of Czar.

1920 The League of Nations founded.

1933 Hitler became Chancellor of Germany.

1939-1945 World War II

1945 First Atom Bomb dropped on Hiroshima (6th Aug.) and Nagasaki (9th Aug.).

1953 Mount Everest conquered (29th May).

1956 Nationalisation of Suez Canal by Col. Nasser (26th July).

1957 Artificial earth satellites (Sputniks I and II) Launched by Russia.

1961 Russia sent Yuri Gagarin into space (12th April); Russia constructed 45 mile long wall dividing East and West Berlin (13th Aug.).

1964 Beginning of the International Quiet Sun Year (1st Jan.).

1966 Tashkent Declaration between India and Pakistan (10th Jan.)

1968 Warsaw Pact intervened in Czechoslovakia (21st August).

1969 Americans land on the Moon (21st July), Gandhi Birth Centenary.

1970 China launched her first satellite on 24th April, Russia's unmanned Luna-16 was successful in bringing back to earth the moon's rock samples (September), Luna-17 reached the moon with moon mobile- 'Lunakhod-I'.

1971—Civil War in Pakistan-East Pakistan declared herself independent; formation of the new state of Bangladesh, China's admission to the U.N.O. (Oct. 26); Indo-Soviet Treaty, Indo-Pak War (Dec. 3-17).

1973—Vietnam peace settlement; End of War in Laos; Geneva Peace Conference on West Asia (Dec.)

1974—Indo-Pak-Bangladesh Tripartite Agreement; War in Cyprus; Asian Games.

1975—International Women's Year; U.S.A. ends involvement in Vietnam; Cambodian Government surrenders to Red forces (17th April), South Vietnam surrenders to NLF and North Veitnamese forces (30th April), Suez Canal reopened; Mozambique achieves Independence (11th Nov.); Surinam achieves Independence; Helsinki Treaty; Angola achieves Independence (25th Nov.).

1976—Indo-Pak Agreement on resumption of diplomatic relations (May); O.A.U. Summit at Port Louis (July 15), Fifth Non-aligned Summit in Colombo opened (July 17), 2nd World Hindi Convention at Port Louis (Aug. 28), Death of Mao-Tse Tung (Sept. 9).

1977—Second ASEAN Conference (Aug.), U.S.A. and Panama reach agreement on control over Panama Canal (Aug. 10); World Conference for Action Against Apartheid (Oct).

1978—India-Vietnam sign four aid and trade agreements (Feb. 26); Isarel mounts invasion of Lebanon (March 15); Military Coup in Afghanistan (April 27), Egypt and Israel reach accord on a peace treaty (Sept. 17), Soloman Islands admitted as the (150th members of U.N.O.; Dominica admitted as the 151st member of the U.N.O. (Dec.).

1979—China and the U.S.A. resume diplomatic relations (Jan. 1), International Year of the Child started, Chinese invasion of Vietnam (Feb.), Egypt-Israel Peace Treaty signed.

1980—Sino-Soviet Treaty of Friendship, Alliance and Mutual Aid signed in 1950 expires (April 11), 22nd Olympics at Moscow (July-Aug.), death of Shah of Iran (July 27), Iraq-Iran War (Sept.-Oct.).

1981—International year for disabled persons started. U.S. to make neutron bomb (Aug. 9), Iran's New President elected (Oct. 2), North-Antigua gains freedom (Nov. 1).

1982—The U. N. adopts declaration of religious freedom (Jan. 6), Military seizes power in Surinam (Oct. 5), Coup in Guatemala (March 23), Argentina seizes Falklands (April 2), President Leonid Brezhnev of USSR dies of Heart attack (Nov. 10).

1983—The Seventh Non-Aligned *Summit opens in New Delhi (March 7), UNCTAD-VI meet* ends its months long session (July 3), Summit at U.N. calls for new economic order (Sept. 30).

1984—35 Nations European Security Conference, Stockholm (Jan-Feb.), U.S. Iraq restore diplomatic relations (Nov. 26).

1985—Replaced by Gorbachev (March 15), Accused in Acquino murder trial acquitted (Dec. 2).

1986—Swedish Prime Minister Mr. Olaf Palme is shot dead (March 1), 7 Commonwealth head meet in London (Aug. 3-5), Harare Non-Aligned Summit (Sept. 2-7), 10th Asiads in Seoul (Sept. 20-Oct. 5).

1987—Seven Developed Nations meet in Venice (June 8-10), Fiji declared republic (Oct. 6), The 2nd National Games opened in Trivendrum by President of India (Dec. 28).

1988—G-7 meet in Toronto (June 22-24), President Zia dies in aircrash near Bahawalpur (Aug. 17), Benazir Bhutto becomes Pakistan Prime Minister (Dec. 4).

1989—More than 80 nations agreement in Helsinki for the protection of Ozone layer (May 5), CHOGM concludes at Kualalampur (Oct. 24), Romania's President and his wife executed (Dec. 21).

1990—African Nationalist Leader Nelson Mandela freed after 27 years of imprisonment, (Feb. 11), Iraqui attack and annexation of Quwait (Aug. 2).

1991—Edith Kreson becomes first woman Prime Minister of France (May 15), Security Council elects Boutras Ghali as the next Secretary General of U. N. (Nov. 22), G-15 Summit at Carakas (Nov. 26).

1992—12 European Countries sign a treaty for unity in Masstricht (Feb. 7), UNCTAD ended in Colombia (Feb. 25), Environment and Development Conference in Tokyo (April 17), Barcelona Olympic (July 25-9th Aug.), Boris Yeltsin's China visit (Dec. 16-20).

1993—Bill Clinton was sworn in as America's President (Jan. 20), Clinton-Yeltsin summit (April 3), U.S.A. and Russia agree for stopping export of missile technology (Sept. 2), New Constitution in South Africa (Nov. 18).

1994—Yadav Kant Silvan new SAARC Secretary General (Jan. 1), G-15 Summit held in New Delhi (Mar. 28–30). 12th Asian Games concluded in Hiroshima (Oct. 16).

1995—SAARC Summit in New Delhi (May 2-4), Myanmar Junta frees Aung San Suu Kyi (July 10), Vietnam becomes the Seventh member of ASEAN (July 28).

1996—Boris Yeltsin elected the President of Russia (July 4), Atlanta Olympics inaugurated (July 19), American President Bill Clinton signed the CTBT (Sept. 23), China will build a second nuclear power plant in Pakistan (Dec. 5).

1997—Kofi Annan of Ghana took office as the seventh U.N. Secretary General (Jan. 1), SAARC Summit held in Male (12–15, May), Russia and NATO sign pact (May 27), G-15 summit held in Kualalumpur in Malaysia (Nov. 3–5).

1998—Vaclav Havel elected the president of Czech Republic (Jan. 20), Miss Trinidad and Tobago's Wendy Fitz William is new Miss Universe; G-15 summit held in Cairo (May 13); G-8 Summit held in Birmingham (May 15–17), Islamic Rule Bill passed in Pakistan National Assembly (Oct. 9), 13th Asian Games ended in Bangkok (Dec. 19).

1999—The eighth round Jaswant-Talbott talks begin (Jan. 29), India and Qatar sign three agreements (April 7), Yugoslavia accepts a peace plan for Kosovo (June 3), G-8 summit calls upon Pakistan to respect LoC in Kashmir and withdraw intruders from Kargil (June 25), Macau is reverted to China by Portugal (Dec. 19-20), Russian President Boris Yeltsin resigns (Dec. 31).

2000—UNCTAD's X Session in Bangkok (Feb. 12–19), Vladimir Putin elected the new President of Russia (March 27), Japan (July 21), 27th Olympiad at Sydney inaugurated (Sept. 15).

2001—American spacecraft NEAR lands on the asteroid EROS (Feb. 13), Dennis Tito returns to earth (May 6), 11th G-15 Summit in Jakarta (May 30 and 31,), Interim Government for Afghanistan (Dec. 22).

2002—Integrated currency of the European Union, 'Euro' comes into force (Jan. 1), Second Earth Summit held in Johannesburg, S. Africa (Aug. 26–Sept. 4), Spanish naval ships capture N. Korean Vessel carrying Scud Missiles (Dec. 9).

2003—World Trade Organization's Ministerial meet at Cancun, Mexico (Sept. 10–14), Severe earthquake brings death and destruction in Iran (Dec. 26).

2004—US spacecraft Rover 'Spirit' lands on the Mars (Jan. 4), 10 new nations join the European Union raising its strength to 25 (May 1), George Bush is re-elected as President of the USA (Nov. 4), The APEC Summit in Santiago, Chile (Nov. 20-21), SAARC Conference of Commerce Ministers (Nov. 23-24), Saudi Arabia recalls its ambassador to Libya in protest against 'Tripoli Plot' (Dec. 22).

2005—Bangladesh Cricket makes history by defeating Zimbabwe and posting its first ever test win (Jan. 10), George W. Bush is sworn in again as the President of America (Jan. 20), Commonwealth Chief Election Officials' 8th Conference in New Delhi (Feb. 24–28), G-77 Summit Conference held in Doha, Qatar (June 15-16), India–ASEAN Summit Meet (Dec. 12).

2006—South Asian Free Trade Agreement—SAFTA among SAARC countries (Jan. 1), South Asian Federation Games opened in Colombo, Sri Lanka (Aug. 18) , Sunita Williams, American astronaut of Indian origin in space shuttle Discovery launched for ISS (Dec. 10), The 15th Asiad comes to a close in Doha with China topping the medals tally (Dec. 15), Saddam Hussein, the former President of Iraq hanged (Dec. 30).

2007—Luiz Inacio Lula sworn-in as *President of Brazil for a second term (Jan. 2), The 14th* SAARC Summit is opened in New Delhi with Afghanistan formally inducted as the 8th member of the regional grouping

(April 3), The final of ICC Twenty-20 World Cup Cricket played at Johannesburg, South Africa, India wins the World Cup (Sept. 24), Former Pakistan PM Benazir Bhutto has been killed in blast (Dec. 27).

2008—India beat Australia by nine runs in the second final of the CB-Tri-Series at Gabba in Brisbane (March 4), Hu Jintao re-elected Chinese President (March 14), US Senate gave final congressional approval to an agreement end the three decade ban on US nuclear trade with India with 86 votes in favour and 13 against it (Oct. 2), UN Convention on Climate Change sets roadmap for Copenhagen meet in 2008 (Dec. 13).

2009—Barack Obama has taken the oath of office and been sworn-in as America's 44th President (Jan. 20), Iraq to reopen notorious Abu Gharib Prison (Jan. 25), UN Conference on Climate Change opens in Copenhagen, Denmark (Dec. 7), China-Kazakhstan gas pipeline inaugurated (Dec. 12).

2010—First Woman Lutheran Bishup Maria Jaspen resign over from her post in Northern Germany (July 17), Ground Zero Mosque wins approval in United States of America (August 3), 19th Commonwealth Games opened in New Delhi (October 3), 16th Asian Games concluded in Guangzhou, China (Nov. 27).

2011—Barack Obama signed debt ceiling bill (Aug. 3), China has conferred its highest Literary award on B.R. Deepak for his book, which is a translation of 88 Classical Chinese poems into Hindi (Sept. 2), Libyan dictator Gaddafi killed (Oct. 20). Kim Jong-Unnamed Military Chief of North Korea (Dec. 31).

2012—Jim Yong Kim chosen to lead World Bank (April 17), The 30th Olympic Games inaugurated in London (July 27), NAM Summit begins in Tehran (Aug. 30), India wins 2012 Under-19 Cricket World Cup (Aug. 26), Nikosazana Dalamini Zuma became the first woman to take office as chair-person of African Union Commission (15 Oct.), Barack Obama re-elected President of America (6 Nov.), U. N. recognizes state of Palestine as an observer state (29 Nov.).

2013—John Kerry sworn in U.S. as new Secretary of State (2 Feb.), Venezuelan President Hugo Chavez dead (6 March), President of Bangladesh Zillur Rahman died (20 March), Former British P. M. Margret Thatcher passes away (8 April), 11th ASEAN Summit in Brunei (10 Oct.), Bharat Ratna Mandela passes away (5 Dec.), Jordan elected to UN Security Council (6 Dec.).

2014—Nepal Supreme Court gives Voters Right to reject Candidates (5 Jan.), Bangla Desh Polls, Sheikh Hasina wins (7 Jan.), Reuven Rivilin elected president of Israel (10 June), Ukraine signs trade pact with E.U. (27 June), Germany emerges champion of FIFA Cup 2014 (14 July), Jokowi wins Indonesia's Presidential Polls (22 July), Joko widodo sworn in as Indonesia President (20 Oct.), WHO declared Nigeria as Ebola free country (20 Oct.), Sweden become the first European Union Country to recognize the state of Palestine (30 Oct.), New tower of world trade centre re-opened 13 years after 9/11 attacks (3 Nov.), G-20 Summit concludes in Brisbane, Australia (17

Nov.), 18th SAARC Summit at Kathmandu, Nepal (26-27 Nov.), India rejects a draft resolution on nuke weapons in UNGA (2 Dec.).

2015—China launched Silk Road Infrastructure Project in North-west Province of Gansu (2 March), Kathmandu-Varanasi-Kathmandu bus service flagged off (7 March), India Iran Ink Chabahar Port deal (6 May), Ameenah Gurib Fakim has appointed as first woman President of Mauritius (1 June), G-7 Summit in Germany (7-8 June), India Kazakhstan signed Five Agreements (8 July), 7th BRICS Summit held in Ufa (9 July), Parliamentry elections in Sri Lanka (20 Aug.), Nepalese Parliament elects K. P. Sharma Oli as New P. M. of Nepal (11 Oct.), United Nations Human Development Report 2015 released (15 Dec.).

2016—Sanotias lifted after Iran Honours all nuclear commitments (17 Jan.), Parliament of Pakistan became first in world to run entirely on solar power (23 Feb.), Htin Kyaw took oath as Myanmar's first elected President (30 March), SCO Summit 2016 concludes in Tashkent (24 June), S.R. Nathan Indian origin President of Singapore passes away (23 Aug.), Maldives quits commonwealth (13 Oct), Donald Trump elected as 45th President of USA (9 Nov.), Paolo Gentiloni appointed as new Italian PM (11 Dec.).

2017—Pakistans bid to join missile technology control regine (12 Jan.), UK's House of Lords gave its final approval on the Brexit bill (13 March), Maggie MacDonnell, a Canadian teacher was named the winner of the annual Global Teacher Prize at a ceremony conducted (19 March), Hassan Rouhani re-elected as President of India (20 May), Sher Bahadur Deuba takes oath as Prime Minister of Nepal (7 June), BRICS Nations sign MoU to facilitate taxation cooperation (27 July), North Korea Carries out H. Bomb Test (3 Sept.), 9th BRICS Summit held in Xiamen China (3-5 Sept.), USAID announces USD 1 million support for ending Tuberculosis Epidemic in India (1 Dec.).

2018—Saudi Arabia allows women to open business without Male consent (19 Feb.), China makes historic move, allows Xi Jinping to remain President indefinitely (12 March), Mauritius to host 11th World Hindi Conference (12 June), North Korea named as Worst-human trafficking country for 16 years (29 June), The United Kingdom has been ranked at the top in the 2018 'Soft Power 30' Index (18 July), The Norwegian Nobel Committee has decided to award the Nobel Peace Prize for 2018 to Denis Mukwege and Nadia Murad for their efforts to end the use of sexual violence as a weapon of war and armed conflict (5 Oct.). 33rd ASEAN Summit was held in Singapore (15 Nov.), International Day for the Elimination of violence against women observed on Nov. 25, 2018 (25 Nov.).

2019—US, Israel withdraw from UNESCO (Jan. 1), First human rights TV channel launched in London (Jan. 15), Abu Dhabi adds Hindi as third official court language (Feb. 10), Benjamin Netanyahu set to win record fifth term in Israel (11 April), UN launches 'Feed Our Future' cinema *ad campaign in India (23 October), Mahindra Rajapaksa* sworn in as new PM of Sri Lanka (21 November), Saudi oil giant Aramco has announced its Initial Public Offering

(IPO) at $ 25·6 billion, which is the world's largest ever (6 December), Former Pakistani President Pervez Musharraf awarded death penalty (17 December).

2020—UK exiled European Union (EU) (31 Jan.), Saudi Arabia ends death penalty for minors (26 April), WHO declares Africa polio free (26 Aug.), Kerala Government and UN Women collaborate for India's first Gender Data hub (24 Dec.).

2021—Donald Trump becomes first US President to be impeached twice (14 Jan.), Joe Biden inaugurated as 46th US President, Kamala Harris sworn-in as first female US Vice-President (20 Jan.), Russia launched First Arctic Monitoring Satellite (1 Mar.), Russia's President Vladimir Putin signs law enabling him to run for President again (6 April), NASA, Axiom announce first private astronaut mission to ISS (13 May), India hosted the virtual 13th BRICS summit (9 Sep.), COP26 Summit held at Glasgow (31 Oct.–12 Nov.), Olaf Scholze took over as Chancellor of Germany (8 Dec.).

2022—Indonesia to build new capital in Nusantara (20 Jan.), QUAD Foreign Ministers' meeting was held in Melbourne, Australia (11 Feb.), Russia invaded Ukraine (24 Feb.), BIMSTEC Fifth Summit took place in Colombo, Sri Lanka (30 March), 14th BRICS Summit held under the Chairship of China (23-24 June), G-7 held in Germany (27-28 June), The 2022 SCO summit was held in Samarkand, Uzbekistan (16 Sep.), India ranks 107th out of 121 countries on Global Hunger Index (15 Oct.), Indian Origin Rishi Sunak becomes UK Prime Minister (25 Oct.), The 2022 G-20 Summit was held in Nusa Dua Bali, Indonesia (15-16 Nov.), CoP-27 takes place in Sharm-El-Sheikh, Eygypt (20 Nov.), Argentina won FIFA World Cup 2022 against France (18 Dec.).

2023—Germany won the 2023 Men's Hockey World Cup (29 Jan.), AUKUS Deal : USA, UK and Australia Agree on Nuclear Submarine Project (13 March), G-7 Summit hosted by Japan, Prime Minister Modi Attends (21 May), Polish Player Iga Swiatek secured her fourth Women's Tennis Association title of the year 2023 (1 Aug.), Spain secured their first FIFA Women's World Cup title 2023 (21 Aug.), 20th ASEAN-INDIA Summit and 18th East Asia Summit held in Jakarta (7 Sept.), 18th G-20 Summit 2023 held in New Delhi and African Union became 21st member of G-20 (9–10 Sept.), India-Argentina have signed 'Social Security Agreement' (3 Oct.), UNICEF celebrates milestone of one million certificaitons on International Day of the Girl Child (3 Oct.), China is constructing the world's largest "ghost particle" detector, the Tropical Deep-sea Neutrino Telescope (TRIDENT) (19 Oct.), Dominica creates world's first Marine Protected Area for Sperm Whales (15 Nov.).

2024—Scientists have uncovered the most ancient skin fossil, dated about 286 million years old. (16 Jan.), Researchers at Stanford University discovered a new virus-like entity called obelisks (6 Feb.), Iran launched of its domestically manufacturing 'Paras 1' remote orbit (March 1), Claudia Sheinbaum elected Mexico's first woman President (3 June), The 50th GT Summit was held at Apulia (Italy) (12-15 June), Bangladesh Prime Minister Sheikh Hasina State Visit of Prime Minister Narendra Modi to India (21-22 June), BIMSTEC Foreign Minister's conference held in New Delhi (11-12 July), Shanghai Cooperation Organisation (SCO) Summit held in Astana Capital of Kazakhstan (3-4 July), President Draupadi Murmu's visit to Fiji, New Zealand and Timor Leste (5–10 August), Shri Narendra Modi is the First Indian PM to visit Ukraine since 1992 (23 August), Typhoon Shanshan Hits Southern Japan (29 August), Dhulikhel Becomes Nepal's First 'Healthy City' and Second Healthiest City in Asia : Who (31 August), Super Typhoon Yagi hits Southest Asia (7 September), Nepal Became 101st members of International Solar Alliance (ISA) (11 September), Algeria joins BRICS New Development Bank (13 September), Angkorwat named most photogenic UNESCO World Heritage Site in Asia (17 September), Sixth QUAD leader's Summit (2024) —Delaware (USA) (22–23 Sept.).

BRICS summit held in Kazan, Russia (22-24 October), UAE's new position in global standards, becomes the first Arab country to join the IEC board (3 November), Donald Trump elected as the new President of America (6 November).

2025—Nigeria officially becomes a partner country of the BRICS block (January 17), Donald Trump sworn in as the 47th President of the United States (January 20), America withdraws itself from WHO and Paris Climate Agreement (January 22), Alexander Lukashenko becomes President of Belarus for the seventh time (January 28), PM Narendra Modi co-chair the ongoing AI Summit in Paris with France (Feb. 12), PM Modi U.S. Visit (12-14 Feb.), India and USA launched the TRUST initiative to enhance co-operation in the recovery and processing of critical minerals (Feb. 15), France to host emergency summit on Ukraine (Feb. 17).

Friedrich Merz Ascends As Germany's New Chancellor (27 Feb.), Donald Trump declared English as the official language of the USA (3 March). Pope Francis, First Latin American Paul died at the age of 88 (21 April), Anthony Albanese re-elected as Australian PM in landslide victory (5 May), Robert Frances Prevost elected the 267th Pope (9 May), World's first commercial scale e-methanol plant begins operations in Denmark (15 May), Kami Rita Sherpa scales Mount Everest for 31st time (28 May), Bangladesh drops 'Father of the Nation' title for Sheikh Mujibur Rehman (6 June), Operation Rising Lion : Israel targets Iranian Nuclear sites in escalated strikes (13 June), Israel and Iran accept ceasefire (June 24).

Important Dates of Indian History

B C.

563 Birth of Gautama Buddha; Nirvana (483 B.C.)

540 Birth of Mahavir; Nirvana (568 B.C.)

327-26 Alexander's invasion of India. It opened a land route between India and Europe

273-232 Asoka's reign

58 Beginning of Vikram Era.

A.D.

300-500 Gupta Dynasty-the golden age of Hindu India.

405-411 Visit of Fahien (Chinese Traveller)

606-647 Harsh Vardhan's reign.

1000 First invasion of India by Mahmud Ghazni

1191 Prithviraj defeats Mohd. Gauri at Ist battle of Tarain.

1192 Mohammed Gauri defeats Prithviraj Chauhan at 2nd battle of Tarain.

1498 Discovery of sea-route to India by Vasco-de-Gama (Portuguese).

1526 First Battle of Panipat; Babar founded Mughal Empire in India.

1600 East India Company established in India (31st Dec.)

1657 War of succession among the sons of Shah Jahan begins.

1659-1707 Reign of Aurangzeb.

1761 Third Battle of Panipat.

1764 Battle of Buxar (Bihar).

1773 Regulating Act.

1833 Macaulay recommended English to be the medium of instruc-tion in India.

1853 First Railway Line opened in India.

1857 Indian Mutiny for independence; Calcutta, Bombay and Madras Universities founded.

1869 Birth of Mahatma Gandhi (2nd Oct.)

1885 Indian National Congress founded

1889 Pt. Jawahar Lal Nehru born (14th Nov.)

1905 Partition of Bengal.

1911 Partition of Bengal revoked.

1919 Jalianwalah Bagh tragedy.

1920 Non-co-operation Movement started by Mahatma Gandhi.

1928 Visit of Simon Commission boycotted.

1929 Resolution passed for Purna Swaraj for India at the Lahore Congress under the presidentship of Jawahar Lal Nehru (31st Dec.).

1930 First Round Table Conference of London.

1937—Provincial Autonomy; Congress forms Ministries.

1942—Arrival of Cripps Mission in India; Quit India resolution passed by Congress.

1943-1944—Netaji Subhash Chandra Bose forms provisional Azad Hind Hukumat.

1947—Division of India; India and Pakistan formed into separate independent Dominions.

1948—Mahatma Gandhi assassinated (Jan. 30).

1949—Cease-fire in Kashmir; Indian Constitution signed and adopted.

1950—India becomes a Sovereign Democratic Republic; Death of Sardar Patel; Dr. Rajendra Prasad elected President of Indian Republic.

1951—First Five Year Plan commenced.

1952—First General Elections in the country; Congress Party comes to power.

1956—States Reorganisation Act.

1957—2nd General Elections in India.

1961—Liberation of Goa (Dec. 18).

1962—Third General Elections in India; Chinese attack on India (20th Oct.).

1964—Death of Prime Minister Jawahar Lal Nehru (27th May), Lal Bahadur Shastri elected as the Prime Minister of India.

1965—Indo-Pak War.

1966—Tashkent Agreement signed between India and Pakistan (Jan. 10).

1967—Fourth General Elections held.

1969—Split in the Indian National Congress; death of President Dr. Zakir Hussain and election of V. V. Giri as President of India.

1971—Mid-term elections for Lok Sabha; Indo-Soviet Treaty (9th Aug), Indo-Pak War (Dec. 3-17) Defeat of Pakistan; Bangladesh formed (Dec. 16).

1972—Reorganization of the North-Eastern region—Meghalaya, Manipur and Tripura became full fledged States and new Union Territories of Arunachal Pradesh and Mizoram came into being (Jan. 20, 21); Shimla Agreement (July 3).

1973—Death of M.S. Golwalker (R.S.S. Chief); Indo-Pak Delhi Agreement (Aug.)

1974—India's Nuclear Blast; 36th Constitution (Amendment) Bill passed by Parliament making Sikkim as an associate State of India.

1975—India lifts World Hockey Cup at Kualalumpur, India enters space age by launching 'Aryabhatta'. Sikkim becomes the 22nd State of the Union; State of Emergency to 'forestall internal disturbances' declared; Censorship imposed on Press.

1976—Four Indian News Agencies changed into a single News Agency 'Samachar'; India announces appointment of an ambassador to China (April 16).

1977—Death of President Fakhruddin Ali Ahmed (Feb. 11); Polling for the Sixth Lok Sabha begins (March 16); Janata Party comes into existence (May 1); Janata Party comes into power; Seventh Finance Commission appointed; N. Sanjiva Reddy elected President of India (July); Farakka Agreement signed with Bangladesh (Nov.).

1978—Inauguration of National Adult Education Programme (2nd Oct.); Central Services Examinations to be in regional languages also-Kothari Committee's recommendations accepted by the Central Government (Oct.); 44th Constitution Amendment Bill, as amended by the Rajya Sabha passed by the Lok Sabha (Dec.).

1979—Agreement between India and Canada on the setting up of Joint Commission for economic trade and technological co-operation; India's Second Satellite Bhaskara launched into space.

1980—Reservation for Scheduled Castes and Tribes in the Lok Sabha and State Legislative Assemblies extended for a further period of ten years by the 45th Constitution Amendment Act. (April 14); Six more commercial banks nationalised (April 15).

1981—Sixth Plan draft finalised fixing the target for growth at 5·2 per cent (23rd Jan.); Rohini Satellite in orbit (May 31); Congress (I) becomes Indian National Congress (July 23), Troposcatter link with Russia (Nov. 2), Bhasker-2 launched in orbit (Nov. 1).

1982—Rajasansi Air Port Amritsar becomes International Air Port (Jan. 3); The 21 members Indian scientific expedition headed by Dr. S. Z. A. Qasim, lands on Antarctica (Jan. 9), INSAT-1-A launched (April 10), India's second expedition reaches Antarctica (Dec. 28).

1983—Communal Riots in Assam on election eve (Feb. 15), India launches Rohini-2 satellite by indigenous launcher built in India named SLV-3-D-2 Rocket (June 12), Madras Atomic Power Project at Kalpakkam becomes critical (July 2), INSAT-I-B launched into Space (Aug. 30).

1984—Rakesh Sharma in orbit (April 2-11), Military action in Punjab (June 2), Smt. Indira Gandhi assassinated (Oct. 31), Sri Rajiv Gandhi becomes Prime Minister of India (Oct. 31), Lok Sabha elections completed and Rajiv Gandhi installed as P.M. (Dec. 31).

1985—6 Nations Summit in Delhi (Jan. 28), Anti Defection Bill Passed and comes into force (Feb.), 'Kanishka' crashes near Ireland (June 22), Punjab Accord signed (July 24), Assam Accord signed (Aug. 15), Elections in Punjab (Sept 25), Barnala Govt. installed in Punjab (Sept. 28).

1986—All three accused in the Indira Gandhi assassination case sentenced to death (Jan. 22), Pope John Paul II the spiritual head of Christians arrives in New Delhi (Feb. 1), International criminal Charles Shobharaj escaped from Delhi's Tihar Jail (March 16), Non-Aligned Foreign Ministers meet in New

Delhi (April 15-19), Agreement on Mizoram signed with Laldenga (June 29), Laldenga is new C. M. of Mizoram, Nicaraguan President visits India (9-11 Sept.), Russian leader Gorbachev visits India (Nov. 27-30), Death of Smita Patil (Dec. 13).

1987—Peru President Garcia visits India (Jan. 23-29), $ 70m. African Fund launched (Jan. 25), 39th International Table Tennis Championships at New Delhi (Feb. 20-March 2), Netherland's P. M. arrives in New Delhi (March 3), Elections held in Kerala, J. & K. and West Bengal (March 23), V.P. Singh resigns as Defence Minister (April 12), Death of former PM Charan Singh (May 29), Venkatraman takes oath as 8th President of India (July 25), Death of Hindi poetess Mahadevi Verma (Sept. 11), Jan Morcha launched by V. P. Singh (Oct. 2).

1988—Andhra High Court finds Chief Minister N. T. Rama Rao guilty in seven cases (Jan. 2), INS Varuna successfully completes its mission (April 15), Joint Parliamentary Committee report on Bofor's deal put on the table of the Lok Sabha (April 26), 'Hindu' publishes several documents on Bofor's payments (June 21-22).

1989—Indira Gandhi murder convicts Satwant Singh and Kehar Singh hanged to death (Jan. 6), Court decides 15 crore Rs. compensation in Union Carbide Case (Feb. 14), Successful launch of 'Agni' (May 22), Nhava Sheva port dedicated to the nation (May 26), V.P. Singh is sworn in as P. M. and Devilal as Dy. P. M. (Dec. 2), Ravi Rai elected Lok Sabha speaker (Dec. 19).

1990—'French Mahotsava' concludes in New Delhi (Jan. 18), Successful launch of INSAT-1D (June 12), President's Rule in Jammu & Kashmir (July 18), P.M. V.P. Singh announced 27 per cent reservation to Backward classes on the basis of Mandal Commission Report (Aug. 6), Successful test of 'Akash' (Aug. 14), Lok Sabha passes Prasar-Bharati Bill (Aug. 30), Further action on Mandal Report stayed by Supreme Court till its final decision (Oct. 1), Chandra Shekhar sworn in as P.M. (Nov. 10).

1991—Thiruvananthapuram upgraded as fifth international airport of the country (Jan. 2), Rajiv Gandhi assassinated in Sriperumbudoor (May 21), Justice J.S. Verma to enquire into Rajiv Gandhi's assassination (May 27), P.V. Narsimha Rao takes over as Union Prime Minister (June 21), I.R.S.. 1-B launched from Baikanoor in U.S.S.R. (Aug. 29).

1992—Rajoli Naval Air Station commissioned in Madras (Mar. 11), U.S. imposes sanctions on ISRO for two years (May 11), Successful test of 'Agni' (May 29), INSAT-2A launched (July 9), Lok Sabha passes Panchayati Raj and Nagar Palika Bills (Dec. 22).

1993—Indo-Bhutan agreement for Sankosh Multi-purpose project (Jan. 4), Panchayat Raj Act effective (April 24), INSAT-2B launched by Arian Rocket from French Guyana (July 23), Digvijay Singh elected Chief Minister of Madhya Pradesh (Dec. 7).

***1994**—25th International Film Festival* in Calcutta (Jan. 10-20), India-China sign MouI on banking ties (Oct. 22), The former President Giani Zail Singh dies (Dec. 25).

1995—Supreme Court includes medical profession within consumers' forum (Nov. 14), INSAT-2C successfully launched from Kouru (French Guyana) (Dec. 7), I.R.S.-1C successfully launched (Dec. 28).

1996—Rajinder Kaur Bhattal takes over as first woman C.M. of Punjab (Nov. 21), M. S. Gill appointed new Chief Election Commissioner (Dec. 11), Indo-Israel Agro Centre opens (Dec. 31).

1997—The first air craft carrier INS Vikrant decommissioned from Indian Navy (Jan. 31), I.K. Gujral takes oath as the Prime Minister of India (April 21), INSAT-2D put into orbit successfully (June 4), Sitaram Kesri elected Congress President (June 12), Dr. K. R. Narayanan elected President (July 18), Mother Teresa passed away (Sept. 5), IRS-1D placed in orbit from Sriharikota (Sept. 29).

1998—Vajpayee sworn in as the Prime Minister (March 19), Three nuclear devices at Pokharan (May 11), India conducts two more nuclear tests (May 13), Surface to air missile Trishul test-fired (Nov. 12), About 209 people killed in Punjab train accident (Nov. 26).

1999—13th Lok Sabha constituted (Oct. 10), Mumbai girl Yukta Mookhey is Miss World (Dec. 5), Indian Airlines flight IC-814 hijacked by terrorists (Dec. 24-25), The hostage passengers released (Dec. 31).

2000—The Kargil Committee submits its report (Jan. 7), India's INSAT-3B launched (March 22), President gives his assent to the Bills relating to the creation of the new states of Uttaranchal, Jharkhand and Chhattisgarh (Aug. 28), Chhattishgarh, the 26th State of India constituted (Nov. 1), Uttaranchal, the 27th State of India constituted (Nov. 9).

2001—Indigenously developed Light Combat Aircraft (LCA) successfully test-flown (Jan. 4), India's Agni-II missile successfully test fired (Jan. 17), The Geosynchronous Satellite Launch Vehicle (GSLV-D1) is successfully launched from Sriharikota (April 18), Sampoorna Grameen Rojgar Yojana launched (Sept. 25), Prevention of Terrorism Ordinance (POTO) issued (Oct. 24), Terrorist Attack on Indian Parliament (Dec. 13).

2002—INSAT-3C satellite launched on an Ariane rocket from Kourou in French Guyana (Jan. 24), Bhairon Singh Shekhawat elected Vice-President of India (Aug. 12), Delhi Metro Rail inaugurated (Dec. 24).

2003—First Pravasi Diwas (NRI Day) was held in N. Delhi (Jan. 9–11), INSAT-3A launched from Kourou, French Guyana (April 10), India's 34th International Film Festival (IFFI-2003) starts in New Delhi (Oct. 9), India launches her satellite Resource SAT-1 with the heaviest ever payload (Oct. 17), Ceasefire on LOC in Jammu & Kashmir (Nov. 25), New anti-defection Bill passed by Parliament (Dec. 18),

2004—India's indigenously built T-90 main battle tank 'Bhishma' inducted into the army (Jan. 7), Dr. Manmohan Singh is sworn in as the Prime Minister of India (May 22), Justice Ramesh Chandra Lahoti takes over as the new Chief Justice of India (June 1), General Budget presented in the Lok Sabha by the Finance Minister Mr. P. Chidambaram (July 8).

2005—Right to Information Act, 2005 comes into force (Oct. 12), India's heaviest yet satellite INSAT-4A launched (Dec. 22), L. K. Advani resigns as President of BJP (Dec. 31).

2006—The Supreme Court formally celebrates Independence for the first time (Aug. 15).

2007—Agricultural Scientist Dr. M. S. Swaminathan is honoured by the Royal Government of Cambodia with Sahametrei Medal (Jan. 2), International Conference on Information and Communication Technologies and Development was held in Bengaluru (Dec. 15).

2008—The European Union (EU) accepts Russia's stand on Georgia (Sept. 8).

2009—Union Cabinet approves Nehru Solar Mission (Nov. 19), India, Canada clinch nuclear deal (Nov. 28), India-Russia nuclear deal signed (Dec. 7).

2010—Allahabad High Court delivers its verdict on Ayodhya (Sept. 30), Nitish Kumar became 32nd Chief Minister of Bihar (Nov. 26).

2011—World's Cheapest Tablet PC Akash launched (Oct. 20), DRDO conducts 5th flight of Rustam-1 (Nov. 11), IFFI begins in Panaji (Nov. 22), Cyrus P. Mistry declare heir apparent of Tata Group (Nov. 23), World Urdu Conference held in Hyderabad (Dec. 30).

2012—India launched Agni-5 missile successfully (April 19), Rajya Sabha passed Amendments to the Central Education Institution Act (April 27), Pranab Mukherjee elected India's 13th President (July 22), Hamid Ansari re-elected India's Vice-President (Aug. 8), India signs relaxed visa Pact with Pakistan (Sep. 9), Ranjeet Sinha became the new Chief of CBI (3 Dec.), Pt. Ravi Shankar Sitar maestro and Nityanand Swami Ist CM of Uttarakhand passes away (12 Dec.), Nainalal Kidwai became the first woman President of FICCI (15 Dec.).

2013—Ashok Kumar Mukharjee became new representative of India in U.N. (13 Feb.), Mohan Para Saran appointed as Solicitor General (13 Feb.), UNESCO declares Nicobar Islands as World Biosphere Reserve (May 31), P. Sathasivam appointed as the Chief Justice of India (June 30), India launches its first Indigenous Air Craft carrier INS Vikrant (12 Aug.).

2014—Largest Solar Power Plant of India launched, in Madhya Pradesh (26 Feb.), Narendra Damodardass Modi took oath as India's Prime Minister (26 May), P.M. dedicated indigenously built largest warship INS Kolkatta to the Nation (16 Aug.), Union Government launched Dot (·) Bharat domain (27 Aug.), P.M. launched Make in India Campaign to make India a Manufacturing hub (25 Sep.), Swachh Bharat Mission launched by Narendra Modi (2 Oct.), Supreme Court sets up Social Bench (3 Dec.).

2015—Indian-origin nurse Subadhra Devi Rai became the first Singaporean to get the prestigious biennial prize since its introduction in 1999 (2 April), Union Cabinet approved rehabilitation Package for Bangladesh enclaues (2 Dec.), S.C. directed State and U.T. Governments to consider acid attack Victims under disabled Quato (7 Dec.), Lok Sabha Passed Arbitration and Conciliation (amendment) Bill 2015 (18 Dec.).

2016—Veteran Singer Ustad Abdul Raswel Khan died (18 Feb.), Fire destroyed Delhi's National Museum of Natural History (26 April), PM launched mega schemes to give 5 crore gas connections free to BPL families (May 1), Bankruptcy Bill Passed *in Parliament (5 May), ISRO Flights* tests Scramjet Rocket Engine (28 Aug.), India carries out surgical strikes on Terror Targets across LoC (29 Sept.).

2017—Union Government clears Coast at Surveillance Project (21 Feb.), The Union Government informed that five Indian cities were included in the Tentative List of UNESCO World Heritage Sities (22 March), K. K. Venugopal appointed as Attorney General of India (30 June), Ram Nath Kovind takes oath as India's 14th President (25 July), U.S. Defence Secretary visits India (26 Sept.), Union Cabinet approves setting up of National Nutrition Mission (2 Dec.).

2018—ISRO again scripts history : Places 100th Satellite into arbit (12 Jan.), HRD Ministry launches second edition of Unnat Bharat Abhiyan (25 April), PM Modi inaugurates Integrated Command and Control Centre of Naya Raipur Smart City (18 June), PM Narendra Modi inaugurates first assembly of International Solar Alliance (5 Oct.), ISRO successfully launches communication satellite GSAT-29 (15 Nov.), Government launched : Mission Raksha Gyan Shakti (27 Nov.).

2019—Lok Sabha passes DNA (use and applicaton) Technology Regulation Bill (Jan. 8), President gives assent to Right of Children to Free and compulsory education (Amendment) Act 2019 (Jan. 10), Rishi Kumar Shukla appointed as CBI Director (Feb. 2), Narendra Modi sworn as the Prime Minister of India (30 May), Public Premises (Eviction of Unauthorized Occupants) Amendment Bill, 2019 comes into force (17 September), Ayodhya final verdict : Ram Temple to be built at disputed Ayodhya site, 5 acres of alternate land for Muslims (11 November), Parliament passes bill to merge Daman and Diu, Dadra and Nagar Haveli UTs (3 December), The Citizenship Amendment Bill, 2019 was passed by Parliament (December 11), The government of India has launched National Broadband Mission (NBM) (December 19), The Central Government has renamed Rohtang Pass as 'Atal Tunnel' (December 26).

2020—General Bipin Rawat took charge as India's first Chief of Defence Staff (CDS) (January 1, 2020), Citizenship Amendment Act came into effect as the central government has issued a notification for the revised citizenship act (January 10, 2020), Union Cabinet approves ordinance to create 'One India, One Agriculture Market' (4 June), Consumer Protection Act, 2019 comes into force (20 July), The first Kisan started from Devlali in Maharashtra's Nashik to Danapur in Bihar's (7 Aug.), Parliament passes Epidemic Diseases (Amendment) Bill, 2020 and Parliament passes Insolvency and Bankruptcy Code (Second Amendment) Bill, 2020 (22 Sept.), P.M. Narendra Modi inaugurates world's longest highway tunnel-Atal Tunnel at Rohtang (3 Oct.), Meri Saheli initiative launched by Indian Railways (30 Oct.), The navies of Japan, India, the US and Australia on started the first phase of four days long Malabar Naval Exercise in the Bay of Bengal (3 Nov.), The National Digital Health Mission will be rolled out across India in January 2021 (9 Dec.), India and Bangladesh reopens Chilahati-Haldibari railway link after 55 years (17 Dec.), PM Modi inaugurates first driverless train of India on Delhi Metro (29 Dec.).

2021—PM Modi to virtually lay the foundation stone for Maharaja Suheldev Memorial in UP (16 Feb.), PM Narendra Modi to get Global Energy and Environment Leadership Award (27 Feb.), PM takes first dose of COVID-19 Vaccine (1 March), Prime Minister Modi launches 'Jal Shakti Abhiyan' (22 March), West Central Railway becomes first fully electrified Railway Zone in India (5 April), The world's first Nano Urea Liquid for farmers across the world was introduced by the Indian Farmers Fertiliser Cooperative Limited (IFFCO) (31 May), Legendary Actor Dilip Kumar Passes Away (7 July), 105th Amendment (2021) Indian Government announced Birsa Munda Jayanti as 'Janjatiya Gaurav Divas' (15 Nov.), Indian Defence Minister inaugurated 'Revamped war Memorial' at Rezang La. (18 Nov.), PM inaugurated Kashi Vishwanath Corridor in Varanasi (13 Dec.).

2022—S. Somnath appointed as the new ISRO Chief (12 Jan.), India's First Cryptocurrency Index has been launched named ICIS (15 Jan.), PM Modi inaugurated World's second tallest statue (216-feet) 'Statue of Equality' in Hyderabad (5 Feb.), Asia's biggest Bio-CNG Plant Gobar-Dhan inaugurate in Indore (19 Feb.), PM Modi inaugurated the Pradhan Mantri Sangrahalaya in New Delhi (14 April), Droupadi Murmu is the second women President of India (25 July), Rajpath's new name is 'Kartavyapath' (8 September), Lt. General Anil Chauhan (Retd.) appointed as new Chief of Defence Staff (30 Sep.), World's tallest Shiva Statue of Nathdwara inaugurated (29 Oct.).

2023—Anil Kumar Lahoti has taken over the charge of new chairman & Executive officer of the Railway Board (1 Jan.), President Droupadi Murmu's first address to the nation on the eve of 74th Republic Day (25 Jan.), Rashtrapati Bhawan's Mughal Gardens renamed as 'Amrit Udyan' (28 Jan.), Surekha Yadav becomes First Loco Pilot in Asia (13 March). The New Parliament House inaugurated on (28 May), Global Gender Gap Report, 2023, India at (127th Place in 146 coountries), (11 June), Chandrayaan-3 was launched from Sriharikota (Andhra Pradesh) 14 July), India's Grandmaster Gukesh D has become as the country's top chess player, surpassing Viswanathan Anand in Aug. 2023 (4 Aug.), The nationwide campaign 'Meri Mati Mera Desh' has been launched to pay tribute to the 'Veers' who laid down their lives for the country (9 Aug.), India has created history as it became the first country to land (Vikram Lander) on the South Pole of the lunar surface (23 Aug.), Jaya Verma Sinha has been appointed as the first woman chairperson and chief executive officer of the Railway Board (31 Aug.), Aditya L1 launched (2 Sept.), 18th G-20 Summit held in New Delhi (9-10 Sept.), PM Vishwakarma Scheme launched and Yashobhoomi Convention Centre inaugurated (17 Sept.), Last sitting of Lok Sabha and Rajya Sabha in old Parliament House (18 Sept.), First sitting of Lok Sabha and Rajya Sabha in New Parliament House (19 Sept.), Nari Shakti Vandan Adhiniyam 2023 (Women' Reservation Bill) passed in Rajya Sabha (21 Sept.), Air Marshal Sadhan S. Nair has become the second woman officer from the medical branch of the Indian Air Force (IAF) (24 Oct.), The Saurauia Punduana, categorized as crtically endangered by the International Union for Conservation of Nature IUCN Red List, has been found for the first time in Manipur's Tamenglong district (29 Dec.).

2024—*Pran Prathistha* was conducted in Ayodhya's Ram Temple (22 Jan.), Uttarakhand government has introduced legislaiton to implement a Uniform Civil Code (UCC) in the state (6 Feb.), PM Modi launches India's first Hydrogen fuel cell Ferry

(1 March), Narendra Modi took oath as Prime Minister of India consecutive third term (9 June), Om Birla elected as 18th Lok Sabha Speaker (26 June), India won ICC Men's T20 World Cup (29 June). PM Narendra Modi's first official visit to Russia in his third term, President Putin presented highest civilian honor of country to PM Modi. (9-10 July), Ratna Bhandar of Puri Jagannath Temples opened after 46 years (14 July), PM Inaugurates 46th session of World Heritage Committee (21 July), Multiple Landslide in Wayanad district, Kerala (30 July), PM paid tribute to Pingali Venkayya on his birth anniversary (2 Aug.), IIT Madras tops NIRF Ranking, 2024 (12 Aug.), PM Modi addresses the Nation on the 78th Independence Day (15th Aug.), India's first Constitution Museum marks 75 years of the Indian constitution (21 Aug.), India launches world' first mobile hybrid rocket : RHUMI-1 (26 Aug.), Prime Minister Modi releases commemorative stamp for 75 years of Supreme Court (2 Sept.), U.P. Govt. to build Vedic-3D Museum in Varanasi (4 Sept.), Port Blair renamed as Sri Vijaya Puram by GoI (13 Sept.), Union Cabinet Accepts the Recommendations on Simultaneous Elections (One Nation One Election-ONOE) (19 Sept.).

Prime Minister Narendra Modi and his Spanish counterpart Pedro Sanchez inaugurate Tata Advanced Systems' facility in Vadodra, Gujarat (29 Oct.), Justice Sanjiv Khanna becomes the 51st Chief Justice of India (11 Nov.), Tabla maestro Ustad Zakir Hussain died in San Francisco (11 Dec.), Former Prime Minister Dr. Manmohan Singh passes away at the age of 92 (27 Dec.).

2025—Dr. V. Narayanan became the new Chairman of ISRO (14 January), 26 January, 2025, the country celebrated the 76th Republic day (26 January), Indian Railways launched 'SwaRail' for seamless travel (31 Jan.), President Droupadi Murmu inagurates National Tribal Festival 'Aadi Mahotsav' in New Delhi (16 Feb.), Gyanesh Kumar was appointed as the next Chief Election Commissioner (17 Feb.), Aadhar Good Governance Portal launched to Enhance Ease of Living and Service Accessibility (28 Feb.). The Government of India has approved the construction of 12·4 km ropeway from Govindghat to Hemkund Sahib Ji in Uttarakhand (6 March), A terror attack occured in the 'Baisaran Meadow' of Pahalgaon, result in loss of 27 Civilian lives (22 April). India has restricted the flow of water of Chenab of the Baglihar and Salal hydro electric dams in Jammu and Kashmir (5 May), Indian armed forces launch 'OPERATION SINDOOR' on nine terror targets of pakistan and pakistan occupied kashmir (7 May). Following the military confrontation between, India and Pakistan after 'Operation Sindoor' both countries agreed to a ceasefire (10 May), Mizoram becomes India's first fully literate state (21 May), India's first Vistadome Jungle Safari train launched in U.P. (26 May), Khichan and Menar Wetlands get Ramsar tag ahead of World Environment Day (5 June), India's 16th census announced for 2027 (16 June), UPSC launches Pratibha Setu to connect top candidates with Private employers (21 June), India to integrate rare blood donar registry with e-Rakt Kosh (24 June).

Indian Towns, Historical Monuments and Places of Interests

Abu Mt. (Rajasthan)—Hill station on the Aravali Range; Dilwara Temples; sacred centre of Jain worshippers; Police Officers training centre.

Adam's Bridge—Very nearly joined to India between two points *viz.* Mannar Peninsula and Dhanushkodi by a line of sandbanks and rocks called 'Adam's Bridge'.

Agra (U.P.)—The Taj Mahal, Lal Kila, Moti Masjid, Dayal Bag.

Ajanta Caves (Maharashtra)—Near Aurangabad. These are famous for wonderful Buddhist cave temples richly ornamented with sculpture and carved with paintings of exceptional skill.

Akshar Dham—It is a renowned temple of Swami Narain sect in Gandhinagar, Gujarat, scene of terrorist attack on Sept. 24, 2002.

Ambala (Haryana)—Junction station; scientific instruments manufacturing centre; glassware, durries, I.A.F. training centre.

Ambernath—Near Mumbai; Medicine, Tools, Prototype factory and a training school attached to it.

Amritsar (Punjab)—On the north-west border of India. Golden Temple; Jallianwala Bagh tragedy on the 13th April, 1919.

Anand Bhawan—One time residence of Pt. Moti Lal Nehru in Allahabad, now dedicated to the Indian National Congress.

Ankleshwar (Gujarat)—Oil has been struck here.

Apharwatt—World's highest skipoint at 13,500 ft. in Jammu and Kashmir which will be linked by Gulmarg gondola through a cable car.

Aurovile—Is an international township built in Pondicherry with the help of UNESCO.

Avadi—Near Chennai in Tamil Nadu is known for heavy vehicles factory; 'Vijayanta' tanks are built here.

Bardoli (Gujarat)—Famous for non-payment of taxes campaign by peasants of Bardoli started by late Sardar Patel.

Bhubaneshwar—The new capital of Odisha, famous for Lingraja Temple. 68th Congress Session held here in Jan. 1964. The resolution on socialism and democracy adopted at this session.

Bongaigaon—It is a place in Asom where the Government of India has decided to establish an oil refinery and petro-chemical complex at a cost of Rs. 197 crores. Also a polyster fibre plant, a kerosene treating unit besides other ancillary units are expected to be established at the complex.

Bokaro—In Jharkhand; known for the fourth steel plant set up in the public sector with Soviet collaboration.

Chandipur—In Orissa, it is a test firing range centre for test firing missiles.

Chittorgarh—Ancient capital and fortress of Udaipur known for Tower of Victory and 'Mira Bai's Temple'.

Chilka—A lake on the East Coast of India on the Kolkata-Chennai line, about 55 miles from Bhubaneshwar by rail. It is an excellent place for migratory birds and sight seeing.

Dandi—Famous for Salt Satyagrah (Dandi March) by Mahatma Gandhi in 12 March, 1930.

Dhanbad (Jharkhand)—Famous for coal mines and the Indian School of Mines. National Fuel Research Institute is situated here.

Dilwara Temples—*Near* Mount Abu (Rajasthan), there are five Hindu Temples constructed here between 11th and 13th centuries A.D.

Elephanta—An island in Bombay harbour, famous for rockcut temples.

Ellora and Ajanta—In Aurangabad (Maharashtra) famous for wonderful Buddhist cave temples richly ornamented with sculpture and carved with paintings of exceptional skill.

Farakka Dam—Constructed over the Ganges in West Bengal. The purpose of this barrage is the only effective way of freeing the Hooghly of its salinity and improving Kolkata's water supply and preventing Kolkata's harbour from silting.

Fateh Sagar Lake (Udaipur, Rajasthan)—A Rs. 14 Lakh solar observatory being set up on an island in this lake. It will be the first of its kind in India and second in the world.

Fatehpur Sikri—23 miles from Agra City, built by Emperor Akbar in 1569.

Firozabad (U.P.)—Famous for glass and glass bangles industry.

Gangotri—It is a mountain peak in the Himalayas. It is also the name of glacier said to be the source of the Ganges.

Gateway of India—In Mumbai harbour (Formerly Bombay Harbour) erected in 1911 on George V's visit to India.

Gol Gumbaz—Largest dome in India at Bijapur (Karnataka).

Golkunda—A ruined city of India about 7 miles west of Hyderabad; formerly there was a diamond mine here.

Gomteshwara (Mysore)—Famous for the 2,000 years old statue of Jain sage carved out of a single stone.

Golden Temple—In Amritsar (Punjab). Sacred to Sikhs.

Haldia (W. Bengal)—Near Kolkata is known as the site where public sector oil refinery has been set up.

Haldighati—A pass in Rajasthan where, in 1576 the brave Rana Pratap faced the Mughal forces headed by Man Singh and Asaf Khan.

Halebid—In Karnataka, 16 km. from Belur, is well known for its elaboratedly sculptured temples of the Hoysala period.

Hampi—Site of ruins of Vijainagar, ancient capital of Vijainagar Empire. It is in Karnataka.

Hanle—A place in Laddhakh in Jammu & Kashmir, world's highest observatory (15000 ft. from sea level) has been established here).

Hilkaka—A 100 square kilometer Enclave near Surankot in Doda district of J & K which remained under the control of terrorists till April 21, 2003 when Indian Army's Romeo Force recaptured it under the *Operation Sarp Vinash*.

Hirakud—In Orissa, known for Hirakud project.

Hubli—A District headquarters in Karnataka. It came into the news when the BJP activist Uma Bharati surrendered in a Hubli Court in connection with a case relating to the national flag at Idgah maidan in 1994.

Indergarh—With the discovery of stone tools of several sizes, evidence of human habitation dating back to at least 100,000 years has been unearthed at Indergarh in Bhanpura tehsil of Mandsaur district (Madhya Pradesh) bordering Rajasthan.

Infosys City—Infosys, the leading IT company of India has developed the Infosys city near Bangaluru, which is the largest campus in the world among IT services companies.

Jalianwala Bagh—A garden in Amritsar; scene of massacre of innocent Indians by the British on 13th April, 1919.

Jamshedpur (Jharkhand)—Centre of Iron and Steel Industry. Tata Iron and Steel Factory is located here.

Jantar Mantar—In Delhi is an observatory constructed in 1724 during the days of Maharaja Jai Singh II of Amber.

Jama Masjid (Delhi)—Built by Shah Jahan; India's biggest mosque.

Kaman—The last Indian post on LOC along the Srinagar--Muzaffarabad route which was opened for bus service on April 7, 2005. The Kaman Bridge crosses the LOC.

Kandla—An important seaport in the state of Gujarat.

Kandhamal—Kandhamal district of Orissa recently witnessed communal-flare-up after a senior leader of an organisation was shot dead triggering reaction against a particular community.

Kangla Fort—The historic fort in Imphal, which remained the seat for Manipur kings for 200 years was handed over to the Manipur Chief Minister by the Director General Asom Rifles in the presence of Prime Minister Dr. Man Mohan Singh on Nov. 20, 2004.

Khadakvasla—Near Pune; National Defence Academy is situated here.

Kargil—A town in Ladakh, the scene of Indo-Pak conflict in 1999.

Kirkee—Near Pune; Institute of Armament Studies and Meteorological Observatory are located here.

Kochi—Kochi in Kerala will have Asia's first sky city for which decks have already been cleared. The project, an eight and a half km hi-tech flyover flanked by a full-fledged township, will be operational in three years' time.

Kodaikanal—Is a town in Tamil Nadu famous for its observatory for the study of Solar Physics.

Korba—Located in Chhattisgarh is the place where a second giant thermal power plant of 1,100 MW capacity is located.

Madhur—An important pre-historical site dating back to 10,000 years in Dharampuri district of Tamil Nadu where a large collection of Neolithic stones dating back to 3,000 B.C. has been excavated throwing light on a Neolithic habitation there.

Mamallapuram—A place in Tamil Nadu, where the Archaealogical Survey of India (ASI) has unearthed remains of 1200-year old Subramanya temple belonging to the Pallava period (8th century A.D.).

Sriharikota—In the Nellore district on the Andhra coast is India's satellite launching centre.

Sunderban—Is a tract of forests and swamps-165 miles long and 81 miles wide fringing the delta of the Ganges. Brahmputra and Meghna rivers in the Bay of Bengal.

Taj Mahal—The white marble mausoleum built at Agra by Shah Jahan in memory of his beloved wife Mumtaz Mahal.

Talchar—In Odisha is known for Atomic Energy Department's Heavy Water Project.

Thumba—Situated near Trivendrum in Kerala State, it is India's first rocket launching centre.

Titagarh—In West Bengal is known for paper manufacture.

Tarapore—Near Mumbai in Maharashtra, is known for India's atomic power station.

Tower of Victory (Chittor Rajasthan)—Famous tower built by Rana Kumbha, the Raja of Mewar, in 1450 A.D. to commemorate his victory over the muslim forces of Malwa and Gujarat.

Trombay—*In* Mumbai, Atomic Reactors.

Gaziabad—*The district Gaziabad* of Uttar Pradesh is the first district in the country to make available electoral roll on website.

INVENTIONS AND DISCOVERIES

Inventions Discoveries	Discoverer Inventor	Country	Year
I. Geographical			
America	Christopher Columbus	Italy	1492
North Pole (Explored)	Robert Peary	U.S.A.	1909
South Pole (Explored)	Amundsen	Norway	1912
Solar System	Copernicus	Poland	1540
Everest (conquered)	Tabie, Junko	Japan	1975
II. Chemistry & Physics			
Electron	J.J. Thomson	England	1897
Dynamite	Alfred Nobel	Sweden	1862
Incandescent Bulb	Edison	U.S.A.	1860
Law of Gravitation	Newton	England	1687
Printing for the blind	Louis Braille	France	1829
Photography	L. Daguerre	France	1837
Photography (Coloured)	Gabriel Lippman	U.S.A.	1857
Photography (Roll Film)	George Eastman	U.S.A.	1888
Radium	Madame Curie	France	1899
Sputniks (Artificial Earth Satellites)	Russian Scientists	Russia	1957
Theory of Relativity	A. Einstein	U.S.A.	1905
Telegraph	Samuel Morse	U.S.A.	1832
Theory of Evolution	Charles Darwin	England	1859
Telephone	Graham Bell	U.S.A.	1876
Wireless (Radio)	G. Marconi	Italy	1896
X-ray	W. K. Rontgen	Germany	1895
III. Mechanical			
Aeroplane	Wright Brothers (William Wright & Oliver Wright)	U.S.A.	1903
Bicycle	Macmillan	Scottland	1842
Dynamo	Michal Faraday	England	1831
Diesel (Heavy oil for Internal combustion Engine)	Rudolf Diesel	Germany	1897

Electric Lamp	Thomas A. Edison	U.S.A.	1879
Electric Washing Machine	Hulxey Machine Company	U.S.A.	1907
Engine (Railway)	Stephenson	England	1814
Fountain Pen	Waterman	U.S.A.	1884
Gramophone	Edison	U.S.A.	1877
Helicopter	Etienne Ochmichen	France	1924
JCB Machine	Joseph Cyril Bamford	England	1945
Locomotive Power of Steam (Principle of Railway Engine)	James Watt	Scottland	1764
Microscope	Z. Jansen	Netherlands	1590
Motorcycle	G. Daimler	Germany	1885
Power-loom	Cartwright	England	1785
Printing Press	Gutenberg	Germany	1455
Pneumatic Tyres	Dunlop	Ireland	1488
Revolver	Colt	U.S.A.	1835
Submarine	David Bushnell	U.S.A.	1776
Sewing Machine	Elias Howe	U.S.A.	1846
Thermometer	Fahrenheit	Germany	1714
Transistor	W. Shockley	England	1958
Typewriter	Sholes	U.S.A.	1868
Television	J. L. Baird	U.S.A.	1944
Telescope	Hans Lippershey	Netherlands	1608
Telstar	U.S. Scientists	U.S.A.	1962
Transistor	Bardeen, Shockley and W. Brattaion	U.S.A.	1948
Vaccination (Small Pox)	Edward Jenner	England	1796
X-ray	Wilhelm C. Roentgen	Germany	1895

Everyday Science

Q. 1. Why does a body immersed in water weight less than it weighs in air ?

Ans. The upward pressure of water called thrust relieves the force of gravity to some extent and thus results in reduction of weight in water as compared to air.

Q. 2. What is the cause of nightblindness ?

Ans. Nightblindness is caused generally due to deficiency of Vitamin 'A'.

Q. 3. What is acupuncture ?

Ans. Acupuncture is an ancient Chinese technique of deadening pain. The underlying principle is that there are about 500 points in the body at which if a needle is pricked, a mumbing effect is experienced which relieves pain.

Q. 4. What is the function of fuse wire in an electric circuit ?

Ans. A fuse is a wire whose resistance is high and melting point is low. In this when the current is strong the fuse wire gets heated up and melts down and thus saves the circuit from getting overheated.

Q. 5. Why are two eyes more valuable than one ?

Ans. We can view the object from two points at once giving us an idea of solidity also and not only of flatness.

Q. 6. Why does a piece of iron get rusted if left exposed in the open?

Ans. Iron piece rusts if left exposed in the open because it reacts with the oxygen in the air, forming iron oxide, a compound of iron, and oxygen.

Q. 7. Why can petrol fire not be put out with water ?

Ans. The temperature of the burning petrol is so high that the water poured on the petrol fire is evaporated before it extinguishes the fire.

Q. 8. Ice packed in saw dust does not melt quickly, why ?

Ans. Saw dust is a bad conductor of heat and protects the ice from the external heat and hence from melting away quickly.

Q. 9. Why do we see rainbow after rain ?

Ans. The water-drops suspended in the air act as a prism and disperse light into seven colours.

Q. 10. How does electric bulb emit light ?

Ans. The electric current passes through a tungsten wire of high resistance, thus it becomes white hot and begins to emit light.

SOME CURIOUS

(The Largest, Longest, Biggest, Highest, Smallest, First etc. in the world)

Air mail, world's first	at Allahabad in Feb. 1911
Archipelago, Largest	Indonesia
Bird, largest	Ostrich
Bird, smallest	Bee Humming Bird

Bridge, biggest in the world	The Danyang–Kunshan Grand Bridge, China (164 km)
City, largest (population)	Tokyo (3,71,94,104)
City, biggest in area	New York (8683 km)
City, highest	Wen Zhuan (China)
Continent, biggest	Asia
Continent, smallest	Australia
Country, biggest	Russia (17,125,191 sq. km)
Country, highest	Tibbet
Delta, largest	Sunderbans (India)
Desert, biggest	The Great Sahara (Africa 3·5 million sq. miles)
Dome biggest	Gol Gumbaz (Bijapur, Karnataka State, India)
Electorate, largest	India (over 91 crores)
Epic, longest	Mahabharat
Genius, world's greatest	Leonardo-da Vinci, painter, sculptor, architect, engineer, scientist etc.
Irrigation Scheme, world's (biggest)	Lloyd Barrage, Sukkur (Pakistan)
Island, biggest in the world	Greenland
Inland Sea, largest	Mediterranean Sea
Mountain, world's highest	Mount Everest (29,028 ft.) Nepal
Museum, world's biggest	Louvre (Paris)
Observatory, highest	Indian Astronomical Observatory Hanle (Ladakh)
Ocean, biggest	The Pacific (16,53,84,000 sq. km)
Park, biggest	Yellow Stone National Park (USA)
Peninsula, largest	Arabia
Smallest country	Vatican City
Planet, biggest	Jupiter
Planet, smallest	Mercury
Planet, farthest (from the sun)	Neptune
Planet, nearest (to the sun)	Mercury
Planet, brightest	Venus
Population, largest (2023)	India (142·8 crore)
Railway Platform, longest	Gorakhpur (India)
Region, world's coldest	Siberia (Verkhoyansk)
Sea bird, largest	Albatross
Stamp, world's first	Penny Black (British), 1840
Statue, world's biggest	Statue of Unity (Sardar Vallabhbhai Patel, 182 Meters, India)
Stupa, world's highest Boddha	Kesariya (East Champaran, Bihar)
Swimming course (longest recognised)	English Channel
Tallest Building in the World	*Burj Khalifa*
Thoroughfare, world's largest	Broadway (New York)
Road Tunnel, longest	Laerdal tunnel (Norway) 24·5 km.
Volcano, highest	Ojasdel Salado, Argentina–Chile (6,885m)

Volcana, Largest	Mauna Loa (Hawai)
Wall, world's longest	The Great Wall of China
Zoo, largest in the world	Kruger National Park, South Africa
Cricket Stadium, Biggest	Narendra Modi Stadium (Motera Stadium, Ahmedabad, Gujarat)
Highest Capital City	La Paz (Bolivia)

Biggest/Highest/Largest/Longest/Smallest in India

The Longest River	The Ganga (2,525 km)
The Longest River of Southern India	Godavari (1465 km)
The Longest Canal	Indira Gandhi Canal or Rajasthan Canal (Rajasthan)
The Longest Dam	Hirakud Dam (Odisha)
The Highest Dam	Tehri Dam on Bhagirathi River (Uttarakhand)
The Highest Lake	Cholamoo Lake (Sikkim)
The Largest Saline Water Lake	Chilka Lake (Odisha)
The Largest Fresh Water Lake	Wular Lake (J & K)
The Largest Artificial Lake	Govind Ballabh Pant Sagar (Rihand Dam)
The Biggest River Island	Majuli, Brahmaputra River (Assam)
The Highest Waterfall	Kunchikal falls, Shimoga (Karnataka)
The Deepest River Valley	Bhagirathi and Alaknanda
The Longest River Bridge	Dr. Bhupen Hazarika Bridge (Dhola-Sadiya, Brahmaputra River) (9·15 km)
The Longest rail-cum-road Bridge	Bogibeel Bridge (Brahmaputra River, Assam)
The Longest Sea Bridge	Rajiv Gandhi Sea Link, Mumbai (Bandra-Worli Sea Link, Mumbai)
The Largest Cantilever Bridge	Rabindra Setu or Howrah Bridge (Kolkata)
The State with Longest Coastline	Gujarat
The Longest River Without Delta	Narmada
The Largest Delta	Sunderbans (West Bangal)
The Longest Railway Platform	Hubballi Railway Station, Karnataka (1·507 metre)
The Highest Road	Road at Khardungla (in Leh-Manali Sector)
The Longest Corridor	Corridor of Ramanatha Swami Temple at Rameshwaram (Tamil Nadu)
The Highest Airport	Leh Airport (Ladakh)
The Largest Zoo	Arignar Anna Zoological Park (Tamil Nadu)
The Biggest Cricket Stadium	Narendra Modi Stadium, Ahmedabad (Gujarat)
The Largest Auditorium	Sri Shanmukhananda Hall (Mumbai)
The Tallest TV Tower	Rameswaram TV Tower (Tamil Nadu)
The Largest Gurudwara	Golden Temple, (Amritsar)
The Largest Cave Temple	Kailash Temple (Ellora, Maharashtra)
The Biggest Church	Basilica of Bom Jesus (Goa)
The Highest Battle Field	Siachen Glacier
The Longest National Highway	NH-44 (Sri Nagar to Kanyakumari)
The Largest Mosque	Taj-ul-Masajid (Bhopal)

The Fastest Train in India	Vande Bharat Express
The Longest Road Tunnel	Dr. Syama Prasad Mukherjee Tunnel (Chenani–Nashri Tunnel, 9·28 km) (J & K) (also Asia's Longest Tunnel)
The Largest Animal Fair	Sonepur (Bihar)
The Largest Cave	Krem Liat Prah, Jaintia Hills (Meghalaya)
The Highest Gateway	Buland Darwaza, Fatehpur Sikri (UP)
The Longest Passenger Train	Vivek Express
The Longest Passenger Train Route	Dibrugarh to Kanya Kumari
Tallest Statue in India	Statue of Unity
Longest Electrified Railway Tunnel	Between Cherlopalli and Rapuru stations (6·6 km) (Andhra Pradesh)

Currencies of Different Countries

Country	Currency	Country	Currency
Australia	Dollar	Sri Lanka	Rupee
Bangladesh	Taka	China; people's Republic	Yuan
Belgium	Euro		
Britain	Pound (Sterling)	Czechoslovakia	Koruna
Burma (Myanmar)	Kyat	Denmark	Krone
Canada	Dollar	France	Euro
Germany	Euro	Pakistan	Rupee
Iran	Toman	Poland	Zloty
India	Rupee	Spain	Euro
Indonesia	Rupiah	Sweden	Krone
Iraq	Dinar	Switzerland	Franc
Italy	Euro	Turkiye	Lira
Japan	Yen	Egypt	Pound
Mexico	Peso	U.S.A.	Dollar
Netherlands	Euro	Russia	Rouble
European Union	Euro	South Africa	Rand

Capitals of Countries

Country	Capital	Country	Capital
Austria	Vienna	Hungary	Budapest
Afghanistan	Kabul	Iran	Tehran
Algeria	Algiers	India	New Delhi
Angola	Luanda	Indonesia	Nusantara
Australia	Canberra	Iraq	Baghdad
Argentina	Buenos Aires	Italy	Rome
Bangladesh	Dhaka	Japan	Tokyo
Belgium	Brussels	Kampuchea (Cambodia)	Phnom Penh
Bolivia	Lapaz		
Bulgaria	Sofia	Korea (North)	Pyong Yang
Bhutan	Thimpu	Korea (South)	Seoul
Brazil	Brasilla	Kenya	Nairobi
Canada	Ottawa	Kuwait	Kuwait
China, People's Republic	Beijing	Laos	Vientiane
		Lebanon	*Beirut*
China (Nationalist)	Taipeh	*Mexico*	Mexico City
		Malaysia	Kualalumpur
Cyprus	Nicosia	Morocco	Rabat

Columbia	Bogota	New Zealand	Welington
Denmark	Copenhegan	Netherlands	Amsterdam
Eire	Dublin	Panama	Panama City
Ethiopia	Addis Ababa	Portugal	Lisbon
Finland	Helsinki	Poland	Warsaw
France	Paris	Sri Lanka	Sri Jayawardenepura Kotte
Germany	Berlin		
Greece	Athens	Sweden	Stockholm
Guatemala	Guatemala City	Switzerland	Berne
Sudan	Khartoum	Ukraine	Kiev
Sierre Leone	Freetown	U.S.A.	Washington
South Africa	Capetown	U.K.	London
Saudi Arabia	Riyadh	Egypt	Cairo
Spain	Madrid	Vietnam	Hanoi
Thailand	Bangkok	Zambia	Lusaka
Turkiye	Ankara	Israel	Jerusalem
Russia	Moscow	Uzbekistan	Tashkent
Azerbaijan	Baku	Kazakhstan	Astana
Moldavia	Kishinev	Belorussia	Minsk
Kirgizia	Frunze	Georgia	Tbilisi
Armenia	Yerevan	Tadzhikistan	Dushanbe
Latvia	Riga	Lithuania	Vilnius
Montenegro	Podgorica	Turkmenistan	Ashkhabad
Myanmar	Naypidaw	Estonia	Tallinn
Mozambique	Maputo	South Sudan	Juba

Important Places Associated with Persons

Places	Persons	Places	Persons
Bardoli	Sardar Patel	Corsica	Napolean Bonaparte
Fatehpur Sikri	Akbar	Jerusalem	Jesus Christ
Kapil Vastu	Gautam, the Buddha	Macedonia	Alexander
Puducherry	Aurobindo Ghosh	Porbunder	Mahatma Gandhi
Shantiniketan	Rabindra Nath Tagore	Talwandi	Guru Nanak

Geographical Surnames

Bengal's Sorrow	Damodar river	City of Seven Hills	Rome
China's sorrow	Hwango Ho river	Land of Rising Sun	Japan
Cockpit of Europe	Belgium	Land of Maple Leaf	Canada
Dark Continent	Africa	Land of White Elephants	Thailand
Emerald Isle	Ireland	Pillars of Hercules	Straits of Gibraltar
Eternal City	Rome	Playground of Europe	Switzerland
Gift of the Nile	Egypt	World's Loneliest Island	Tristan De Cunha (Mid Atlantic)
Hermit Kingdom	Korea		
Key to Mediterranean	Gibraltar		
Land of the Midnight Sun	Norway		

BOOKS AND AUTHORS

Books	Authors
A bend in the River	V. S. Naipal
A New Deal for Asia	Mahathir Mohammad (PM of Malaysia)
An Equal Music	Vikram Seth
Asian Drama	Gunnar Myrdal
Ain-e-Akbari	Abul Fazal
Alice in Wonderland	Lewis Carrol
Affluent Society	J. K. Galbraith
Arthashastra	Kautilya
Abhijnan Shakuntalam	Kalidas
Agni Pariksha	Acharya Tulsi
Agni Veena	Kazi Nazurul Islam
Anna Karenina	Tolstoy
August Coup, The	Mikhail S. Gorbachov
A Pair of Blue Eyes	Thomas Hardy
A Passage to India	E.M. Forster
Bhagwad Gita, Mahabharat	Veda Vyas
Bliss was it in that Dawn	Minoo Masani
Bihari Satsai	Bihari
Bharat Bharati	Maithili Saran Gupta
Charitraheen	Sarat Chandra Chatterjee
Chittirappavai	P.V. Akilandam
Cosmic Reality	Lajja Ram
Divine Comedy	Dante
Discovery of India	Jawahar Lal Nehru
Death of a City	Amrita Pritam
Decline and Fall of Roman Empire	Gibbon
Das Capital	Karl Marx
Descent of Man	Charles Darwin
Devi-The Bandit Queen	Richard Shears and Isoble Gidli
Death, The Supreme Friend	Kaka Saheb Kalelkar
Disgrace	J. M. Coetzee
Experiments with Untruth	Michael Anderson
Eternal India	Mrs. Indira Gandhi
End of an Era, The	C. S. Pandit
Fasting, Feasting	Anita Desai
Freedom from Fear	Aung San Suu Kyi
Glimpses of World History	Jawahar Lal Nehru
Glimpses of India	Humayun Kabir
Gitanjali	Rabindra Nath Tagore
Golden Threshold, Broken Wing	Sarojini Naidu
Godan, Rang Bhumi, Kaya Kalp	*Prem Chand*
Gulag Archipelago	Alexander Solzhenitsyn
Gurusagaran	O. P. Vijayan

Harsha Charit	Bana Bhatta
Hindu View of Life	Dr. S. Radhakrishnan
History of Western Philosophy	B. Russel
Human Knowledge	B. Russel
India Wins Freedom	Abul Kalam Azad
Indian Philosophy	Dr. S. Radhakrishnan
I Follow the Mahatma	K. M. Munshi
Indian War of Independence	V. D. Savarkar
If I am Assassinated	Zulfikar Ali Bhutto
Indira Gandhi	Pupul Jaykar
Jobs for Millions	V. V. Giri
Kamayani, Prem Pathic, Ajatshatru	Jai Shanker Prasad
Khizr Tiwana	Dr. Ian Talbot
Life Divine	Sri Aurobindo
Lenin in Zurich	Alexander Solzhenitsyn
Last Days of Netaji	G. D. Khosla
Les Miserables	Victor Hugo
Mahabharat	Veda Vyas
Mein Kempf	Hitler
My Childhood Days	Taslima Nasreen
My Days	R. K. Narayan
My Experiments with Truth	Mahatma Gandhi
My Music My Life	Pt. Ravi Shankar
My own Boswell	M. Hidayatullah
My Presidential Years	R. Venkataraman
Murder in the Cathedral, Waste Land	Eliot, T. S.
Mrityunjaya	Birendra Kumar Bhattacharya
Naganand	King Shri Harsha
Neeti Shatak	Bharthari
Nehru and His Vision	Dr. K. R. Narayanan
Odyssey, Illiad	Homer
Origin of Species, Descent of man	Charles Darwin
Oil	Jack Anderson
Panchtantra	Vishnu Sharma
Paradise Lost	John Milton
Raghuvansha	Kalidas
Rajtarangini	Kalhana
Ramayana	Valmiki (in Sanskrit)
Ram Charit Manas, Vinay Patrika	Tulsi Das
Revenge and Reconciliation	Raj Mohan Gandhi
Shakuntla	Kalidas
Satanic Verses	Salman Rushdie
Shah Nama	Firdausi
Saket, Yashodhara, Bharat Bharati	Maithili Sharan Gupta
Social Contract	Rousseau
Speed Post	Shobha De

The God of Small Things	Arundhati Roy
The Light that Failed	Rudyard Kipling
The Ground Beneath Her Feet	Salman Rushdie
The City of Joy	Dominique Lapierre
The Greater Common Good	Arundhati Roy
The Tin Drum	Guenter Grass
The Train to Pakistan	Khushwant Singh
War and Peace	Tolstoy
Wake up India	Annie Besant
War of Indian Independence	Vir Savarkar
The Martyr	Kuldeep Nayyar
Interpreter of Maladies	Jhumpa Lahiri
Across Black Waters	Mulk Raj Anand
Fury	Salman Rushdie
Satwan Lok	P. L. Gautam
Bradman's Best	Rolland Perry
Wings of Fire	Dr. A.P.J. Abdul Kalam
Ignited Minds	Dr. A.P.J. Abdul Kalam
Step Across the Line	Salman Rushdie
Life of Pi	Yann Martel
Living History	Hillary Clinton
Vernon God Little	DBC Pierre
Elizabeth Costello : Eight Lessons	J. M. Coetzee
Straight From the Heart	Kapil Deo
Envisioning an Empowered Nation	Dr. A.P.J. Abdul Kalam
My Life	Bill Clinton
Magic Seeds	V. S. Naipaul
To a Hunger Free World	Dr. M. S. Swaminathan
The Line of Beauty	Alan Hollinghurst
Pratham Aalo	Sunil Gangoupadhyaya
Small Island	Andrea Levy
The Argumentative Indian	Dr. Amartya Sen
The Sea	John Banville
Blood Brothers	M. J. Akbar
Ayodhya, 6th December, 1992	P. V. Narasimha Rao
Indira Gandhi	Inder Malhotra
Kargil : From Surprise to Victory	V. P. Malik
God's Little Soldier	Kiran Nagarkar
Indian Summers	John Wright
In the Line of Fire : A Memoir	Parvez Musharraf
Fireproof	Raj Kamal Jha
Inspite of the Gods	Edward Luis
Mohan Das	Rajmohan Gandhi
Peeling the Onion	Gunter Grass
Romance with Life	Dev Anand
India's New Middle Class	Leela Fernandis

A Mission in Kashmir	Andrew Whitehead
Let Us Kill Gandhi	Tushar A. Gandhi
My Country My Life	L. K. Advani
Superstar India	Shobha De
Jyoti Punj	Narendra Modi
The Enchantress of Florence	Salman Rushdie
Sea of Poppies	Amitav Ghosh
From Ganges to the Mediterranean	Dr. Vidya Niwas Misra
The White Tiger	Arvind Adiga
Wedding Album	Girish Karnard
Democracy and Human Development in India	Naresh Gupta
Best Friends Forever	Jennifer Weiner
The Idea of Justice	Amartya Sen
Humbling	Philip Roth
The Museum of Innocence	Orphan Pamuk
The Year of the Flood	Margaret Atwood
Five Point Someone	Chetan Bhagat
The Maruti Story	R.C. Bhargava
A. R. Rahman : The Musical Storm	Kamini Mathai
Songs of Blood and Sword	Fatima Bhutto
Wide Angle	Anil Kumble
The Nature of Philosophy	Daya Krishna
On Nuclear Terrorism	Michael Lervi
The Red Sari	Javier Moro
You can Sell	Shiv Kheda
The Scientific Indian	Dr. APJ Abdul Kalam and Y. S. Rajan
The Grand Design	Stephen Hawking and Leonard Mlodinow
Of Thee I Sing	Barack Obama
Convenient Action-Gujarat's Response to Challenges of Climate Change	Narendra Modi
Mysteries of Vedic Face Reading	Hrishikesh Dubey
Quest for Exceptional Leadership	Ravi Chaudhary
M16- The History of the Secret Intelligence Service	Keith Jeffery
The Emperor of all Maladies : A Biography of Cancer	Siddhartha Mukherjee
Ross Masaud	Hakim Syed Zillur Rehman
Controversially Yours	Shoaib Akhtar and Anshu Dogra
The Wandering Falcon	Jamil Ahmad
The Promise	Damon Galgut
Sunrise Over Ayodhya : Nationhood in Our Times	Salman Khurshid
Tomb of Sand	Geetanjali Shree
The Girl in Room 105	Chetan Bhagat
The Seven Moons of Maali Almeida	Shehan Karunatilake
The Education of Yuri	Jerry Pinto
Ambedkar : A Life	Shashi Tharoor

Space (Biography)	Prince Harry
Becoming	Michelle Obama
Ed Finds a Home	Alia Bhatt
I have the Streets : A Kutti Cricket Story	R. Ashwin and Sidharth Monga
A Fly on the RBI Wall	Alpana Killawala
The winner's Mindset	Shane Watson
75 Great Revolutionaries of India	By Bhim Singh, Member of Rajya Sabha
India @ 100 : Envisioning Tomorrow's Economic Power house	Prof. K.V. Subramaniam
Call of the Gir	Parimal Nathwani, member of Rajya Sabha
Breaking Rocks and Barriers	Sudipta Sengupta

United Nation Organisation

Origin of the U.N.O.—The U.N.O. came into existence in 1945. Its Charter was signed on the 26th of June, 1945. It came into force on Oct. 24, 1945.

Charter of the U.N.O.—The Charter is the constitution of the U.N.O.

Aims and Objects—1. To maintain peace and security in the world, 2. To develop friendly relations among nations, 3. To work together to remove poverty, disease and illiteracy in the world and to encourage respect for each other's rights and freedom, 4. To be a centre for helping nations to achieve these goals.

Headquarters of the U.N.O.—New York.

Flag of the U.N.O.—White U.N. emblem is superimposed on light blue background. The emblem consists of the global map projected from the North Pole and embraced in twin olive branches.

Languages—The official languages of the U.N.O. are English, French, Chinese, Russian, Arabic and Spanish but the working languages are English and French only.

Main Organs of the U.N.O.—1. General Assembly, 2. Security Council, 3. Economic and Social Council, 4. Trusteeship Council, 5. International Court of Justice, 6. Secretariat.

The membership of U.N.O. reached 193, last member is South Sudan.

Specialized Agencies of the U.N.O. with their Headquarters

Agencies	**Headquarters**
Food and Agricultural Organisation (FAO)	Rome
International Labour Organisation (ILO)	Geneva
World Health Organisation (WHO)	Geneva
United Nations Educational Scientific and Cultural Organisation (UNESCO)	Paris
International Bank for Reconstruction and Development (IBRD) or World Bank	Washington
International Monetary Fund (IMF)	Washington
International Finance Corporation (IFC)	Washington
International Civil Aviation Organisation (ICAO)	Montreal

International Telecommunication Union (ITD)	Geneva
World Meteorological Organisation (WMO)	Geneva
United Nations International Children's Emergency Fund (UNICEF)	New York
Inter-governmental Maritime Consultative Organisation (IMCO)	London
International Atomic Energy Agency (IAEA)	Vienna
Technical Assistance Administration (TAA)	
Economic and Social Commission for Asia and the Pacific (ESCAP)	Bangkok
United Nations High Commission for Refugees (UNHCR)	Geneva

NATIONAL SYMBOLS

National Emblem—In the National Emblem, adopted by the Government of India from the Sarnath Lion Capital of Ashoka on January 26, 1950, only three lions are visible, the fourth being hidden from view. The wheel appears in relief in the centre of the abacus with a bull on the right and a horse on the left. The bell-shaped lotus has been omitted. The words "Satyameva Jayate" meaning—"Truth alone triumphs", are inscribed below the Emblem in Devnagri script.

National Flag—The National Flag of India is a horizontal tricolour of deep saffron (Kesari), white and dark green in equal proportion. In the centre of the white band there is a wheel in navy blue to represent the Chakra which indeed symbolises the Dharam Chakra.

Use of Flag—A pamphlet entitled Flag Code—India, has been issued by the Government of India to ensure the proper use and display of the Flag.

National Anthem—Rabindra Nath Tagore's song 'Jana-gana-mana' was adopted as the National Anthem of India on January 24, 1950.

National Song—Bankim Chandra Chatterjee's 'Vande Matram' which was a source of inspiration to the people in their struggle for freedom, has an equal status with 'Jana-gana-mana.

National Bird, Flower and Animal of India—Peacock, Lotus and Tiger respectively.

STATES OF INDIA

(Capitals, Principal Languages)

States	Capitals	Principal Languages
Andhra Pradesh	Amaravati	Telugu and Urdu
Arunachal Pradesh	Itanagar	Monpa, Adi, Nissi etc.
Assam	Dispur	Assamese and Bengali
Bihar	Patna	Hindi

Chhattisgarh	Raipur	Hindi
Goa	Panaji	Konkani
Gujarat	Gandhi Nagar	Gujarati
Haryana	Chandigarh	Hindi
Himachal Pradesh	Shimla	Hindi and Pahari
Jharkhand	Ranchi	Hindi
Kerala	Thiruvananthapuram	Malayalam
Karnataka	Bengaluru	Kannada
Madhya Pradesh	Bhopal	Hindi
Maharashtra	Mumbai	Marathi
Meghalaya	Shillong	Khashi, Jaintia and Garo
Manipur	Imphal	Manipuri
Mizoram	Aizawl	Mizo and English
Nagaland	Kohima	Naga, Assamese and English
Odisha	Bhubaneshwar	Odiya
Punjab	Chandigarh	Punjabi
Rajasthan	Jaipur	Hindi, Rajasthani
Sikkim	Gangtok	Sikkimese and Gorkhali
Tamil Nadu	Chennai (Madras)	Tamil
Telangana	Hyderabad	Telgu and Urdu
Tripura	Agartala	Bengali, Tripuri and Manipuri
Uttar Pradesh	Lucknow	Hindi
Uttarakhand	Dehradun	Hindi
West Bengal	Kolkata	Bengali

Union Territories

Andaman and Nicobar Islands	Port Blair	Hindi, Nicobarese, Bengali, Malayalam, Tamil, Telugu
Chandigarh	Chandigarh	Hindi, Punjabi, English
Dadar Nagar Haveli and Daman and Diu	Daman	Gujarati, Hindi
National Capital Territory of Delhi	Delhi	Hindi, Punjabi and Urdu
Lakshadweep	Kavaratti	Malayalam
Puducherry	Puducherry	Tamil, Telugu, Malayalam, English and French.
Jammu & Kashmir	Srinagar	Kashmiri, Dogri, Urdu, Dardi & Pahari
Ladakh	Leh	Ladakhi, Purgi and *Balti*

* *Andhra Pradesh* will have 3 state capital namely–Executive–Visakhapatnam, Legislative–Amaravati, Judicial–Kurnool.

Population of India : Census–2011

The population of the country as per the provisional figures of census 2011 is 1,21,08,54,977 of which 62,32,70,258 are males and 58,75,84,719 (48·46%) are females. The final figures of census 2011 were released in New Delhi on January 7, 2014 by RGI Shri C. Chandramouli.

The major highlights of the census 2011 (provisional figures) are as under—

- The population of India has increased by more than 181 million during the decade 2001–2011.
- Percentage growth in 2001–2011 is 17·7%.
- 2001–2011 is the first decade (with the exception of 1911–1921) which has actually added lesser population compared to the previous decade.
- Uttar Pradesh (19,98,12,341) is the most populous state in the country followed by Maharashtra with 11,23,74,333.
- The percentage decadal growth rates of the six most populous states were declining during 2001–2011 compared to 1991–2001.
  - Uttar Pradesh (25·85% to 20·2%).
  - Maharashtra (22·73% to 16·0%).
  - Bihar (28·62% to 25·4%).
  - West Bengal (17·77% to 13·8%).
  - Andhra Pradesh (14·59% to 11·0%).
  - Madhya Pradesh (24·26% to 20·3%).
- During 2001–2011, as may 25 States/UTS with a share of about 85% of the country's population registered an annual growth rate is less than 2% is compared to 15 States/UTS with a share of about 42% during the period 1991–2001.
- The total number of children in the age-group 0–6 is 16,44,78,150.
- Uttar Pradesh (29·7 million), Bihar (18·6 million), Maharashtra (12·8 million), Madhya Pradesh (10·5 million) and Rajasthan (10·5 million) constitute 52% children in the age group of 0–6 years.
- Overall sex ratio at the national level has increased by 10 points to reach **943** the census 2011 as against 933 in census 2001. This is the highest sex ratio recorded since census 1971 and a shade lower than 1961.
- Kerala with 1084 has the highest sex ratio followed by Puducherry with 1038, Daman & Diu has the lowest sex ratio of 618 (Provisional).
- Child sex ratio (0–6 years) is 914 (Provisional).
- Mizoram has the highest child sex ratio (0–6 years) of 971 followed by Meghalaya with 970. Haryana is at the bottom with ratio of 830 followed by Punjab with 846 (Provisional).
- Literacy rate has gone up from 64·83 per cent in 2001 to 73·0 per cent.

◯ ◯ CONSTITUTION OF INDIA ◯ ◯

Preamble to the Constitution

We the people of India, having solemnly resolved to constitute India into a Sovereign Socialist Secular Democratic Republic and to secure to all its citizens;

JUSTICE, Social, economic and political.

LIBERTY of thought, expression, belief, faith and worship.

EQUALITY of status and of opportunity; and to promote among them all.

FRATERNITY assuring the dignity of the individual and unity and integrity of the Nation.

In our Constituent Assembly this twenty-sixth day of November, 1949, do hereby adopt, enact and give to ourselves this Constitution. The Constitution came into force on January 26, 1950.

Salient Features of the Constitution

1. The Constitution of India is a written and comprehensive document with 395 Articles and 12 Schedules.
2. India is a Sovereign Socialist Secular Democratic Republic.
3. It establishes a parliamentary system of government.
4. It guarantees Fundamental Rights to all citizens of India.
5. It lays down the 'Directive Principles of State Policy' for the guidance of legislatures and the executive of the country.
6. It establishes a federation with strong unitary feature.
7. It provides for an independent judiciary with Supreme Court as the highest court of appeal.
8. It introduces universal adult franchise.
9. It recognises only single citizenship.
10. It incorporates Fundamental Duties of citizens.
11. It establishes a federal political structure with wide unitary features.

Fundamental Rights

1. Right to Equality	1. Equality before Law 2. Social equality 3. Equality of opportunity in public appointment
2. Right to Freedom	Freedom of Speech and Expression, Assembly, Association, Movement, Residence, acquisition and disposition of property. Right to practise any profession or to carry on any occupation, trade or business. Provisions of free and compulsory education *to all children of the age of six to fourteen years.**

---

* Added by 86th Constitution (Amendment) Act, 2002.

3.	Right against exploitation	Right forbids slave traffic in human beings, beggary in any form and forced labour.
	(a) State can enforce	Compulsory military training and military and industrial conscript.
4.	Right to Freedom of Religion	Freedom of religion allows everyone to entertain any notion to exhibit his sentiments in such form of worship, but not injurious to the equal rights of others, all subject to public order, morality and health.
5.	Cultural and Educational Rights	Any section of citizens having a distinct language script or culture of its own have the right to conserve the same.
6.	Right to Constitutional Remedies	Enforceable by the Supreme Court and the High Courts.

Indian Constitution (Drafting Committee) (Constituted on 28.8.1947)

1. Chairman	Dr. B. R. Ambedkar
2. Members	1. N. Gopalasamy Ayyangar
	2. Allady Krishnasamy Ayyar
	3. K. M. Munshi
	4. Md. Sadulla
	5. B. L. Mitter (Resigned) Madhava Rao
	6. Dr. K. P. Kaitan (Died)
	T. T. Krishnamachari
Constitutional Advisor	B. N. Rao

Parliament

It consists of two Houses—(1) Lok Sabha (Lower House) and (2) Rajya Sabha (Upper House) and the President.

The Presiding officer of the Lok Sabha is the Speaker and that of the Rajya Sabha is Chairman. The Vice-President of India is the ex-officio Chairman of the Rajya Sabha.

Executive

President is the head of the State. He is advised by a Council of Ministers headed by the Prime Minister. The Council of Ministers is responsible to the Lok Sabha.

Supreme Court

It is the highest Court of India. It has original, appellate and advisory jurisdictions. In appionment of the Chief Justice of India, President can consult such Judges of the Supreme Court and the High Court as he thinks appropriate. The present strength of the apex court is 34, including the Chief Justice of India.

* Chief Justice of India Salary—₹ 2,80,000 per month and Judges of the Supreme Court Salary ₹ 2,50,000 per month.

State Judiciary

High Court

1.	High Court	Chief Justice and Judges
2.	Appointed by	The President of India
3.	Term	Till the age of 62 years
4.	Jurisdiction	One or more States/Union Territories
5.	Powers Original	Between State and Citizens
	Appellate	Against the judgement of subordinate courts
6.	Guardian of the Constitution	Enforcement of law declared by it.
7.	Salary per month	
	Chief Justice	₹ 2·50 lakh
	Judges	₹ 2·25 lakh

State Administrative Tribunal

1.	Chairman (cadre)	High Court Judge
	Vice-chairman (cadre)	Dt. Judge
	Member	Administrative Service Member
2.	Term	5 years (or) 62 years
3.	Appointed by	Governor of the State
4.	Jurisdiction Original	Between State and State Service personnel

High Courts in India

	Name	Jurisdiction
1.	Allahabad H.C. (1866) Bench : Lucknow	Uttar Pradesh—Prayagraj
2.	Karnataka H.C. (1884)	Karnataka—Bengaluru
3.	Mumbai H.C. (1862) Bench : Aurangabad Nagpur Goa	Maharashtra, Goa, Dadra Nagar Haveli and Daman Diu—Mumbai
4.	Kolkata H.C. (1862)	West Bengal, Andaman & Nicobar Islands
5.	Punjab and Haryana H.C. (1947)	Haryana & Punjab and Chandigarh–Chandigarh
6.	Orissa H.C. (1948)	Odisha—Cuttak
7.	Sikkim H.C. (1975)	Sikkim—Gangtok
8.	Guwahati (1948) Bench : Kohima Aizawl Itanagar	Assam, Arunachal Pradesh, Nagaland and Mizoram
9.	Telangana (2019)	Telangana—Hyderabad
10.	Madhya Pradesh H.C. (1936) Bench : Indore : Gwalior	Madhya Pradesh—Jabalpur
11.	Rajasthan H.C. (1949)	Rajasthan—Jodhpur
12.	*Kerala H.C. (1956)*	*Kerala & Lakshadweep—Kochi*
13.	Chennai H.C. (1862)	Tamil Nadu & Puducherry—Chennai

14.	Uttarakhand (2000)	Uttarakhand—Nainital
15.	Delhi (1966)	Delhi State—New Delhi
16.	Patna H.C. (1916)	Bihar—Patna
17.	Chhattisgarh (2000)	Chhattisgarh—Bilaspur
18.	Gujarat H.C. (1960)	Gujarat—Ahmedabad
19.	Jharkhand (2000)	Jharkhand—Ranchi
20.	Himachal Pradesh (1971)	Himachal Pradesh—Shimla
21.	Jammu and Kashmir, Ladakh (1928)	Jammu and Kashmir and Ladakh—Srinagar (Summer) and Jammu (Winter)
22.	Tripura (2013)	Tripura—Agartala
23.	Manipur (2013)	Manipur—Imphal
24.	Meghalaya (2013)	Meghalaya—Shillong
25.	Andhra Pradesh (2019)	Andhra Pradesh—Amaravati

Important Amendments of the Constitution

The Constitution (1st Amendment) Act–1951—This amendment added Article, 15(4) and Article, 19(6) and brought changes in the right to private property in pursuance with the decision of Supreme Court concerning fundamental rights. Ninth Schedule to the constitution was also added by it.

The Constitution (21st Amendment) Act, 1967—Sindhi Language was included as 15th regional language in the Eighth Schedule.

The Constitution (42nd Amendment) Act, 1976—The Act introduced comprehensive changes in the constitution some of which are as follows :

(i) Provision of Fundamental duties. (ii) Directive Principles made justiceable and given precedence over Fundamental Rights. (iii) Division of Jurisdiction between the Supreme Court and the High Courts in the matter of determination of the constitutional validity of Central and State laws. (iv) Limitation of the jurisdiction of High courts in certain respects (v) Provision for creation of Administrative Tribunals for adjudication for Service matters. (vi) Inclusion of education and certain other subjects in the concurrent list (vii) provision for dealing with antinational and communal activities (viii) Provision for amending Article 368 of the constitution to give emphasis on the mutability of the Constitution and every part thereof.

The Constitution (43rd Amendment) Act, 1977—The President gave assent to the Constitution (43rd Amendment) Act on April 13, 1978 which repealed the obnoxious provisions of the Constitution (42nd Amendment) Act passed during the emergency.

The Constitution (44th Amendment) Act, 1978—This Amendment reverses many of the provisions of the 42nd Amendment and also makes far reaching changes in many of the provisions of the Constitution. The chief of which are as follows :

(i) The right to property has been deleted from the list of Fundamental Rights. It has now become an ordinary legal right.

(ii) The amendment provides that the fundamental right to life and liberty cannot be demolished even during the operation of emergency.

(iii) Another important provision of the amendment is article 361-A. The right of information media, especially the press has been guaranteed to report freely and without censorship the Proceedings in Parliament and State Legislatures.

The Constitution (52nd Amendment) Act, 1985—Crossing the floor or defection has been prohibited by this amendment. If an elected representative changes his party he would lose his seat in the State/Central legislature. However, in case atleast 1/3 members of a party change affiliation, it shall not be treated as defection. It will be treated as a split. A nominated or an independent representative can- not join any party 6 months after his/her nomination or election without losing his/her seat.

The Constitution (55th Amendment) Act, 1986—Arunachal Pradesh was conferred statehood.

The Constitution (56th Amendment) Act, 1987—Hindi version of the Constitution accepted as authoritative.

The Constitution (57th Amendment) Act, 1987—It conferred statehood on Goa.

The Constitution (58th Amendment) Act, 1987—It provides for reservation of seats in the legislatures of 4 north-eastern States of Arunachal, Meghalaya, Mizoram and Nagaland.

The Constitution (59th Amendment) Act, 1988—It empowers the Government to declare Emergency in Punjab and extend President's Rule to 3 years.

The Constitution (60th Amendment) Act, 1988—The state governments have been empowered under this Act to increase the professional tax from ₹ 250 to ₹ 2500 per annum.

The Constitution (61st Amendment) Act, 1988—Voting age in general elections is reduced from 21 to 18 years.

The Constitution (62nd Amendment) Act, 1989—The reservation of seats for SC/ST and the Anglo-Indian Community by nomination in Legislature is increased for other ten years *i.e.*, up to Dec. 20, 1999.

The Constitution (63rd Amendment) Act, 1990—This Act omitted Article 359A which was inserted by 59th Constitution Amendment Act.

The Constitution (64th Amendment) Act, 1990—The Act extended President's rule in Punjab for another six months.

State Public Service Commission

1.	State Public Service Commission	Chairman and Members
2.	Appointed by	The Governor of the State
3.	Tenure	Six years or Sixty-two years of age whichever is earlier
4.	Qualification	Must have held office for atleast ten years under Union or State Government
5.	Duties	To conduct examinations for appointment under State Government Service
	Consultation	To advise on service matters consulted by the Governor of the State regarding recruitment, promotion, disciplinary action referred to by the State Government

The Constitution (65th Amendment) Act, 1990—This Act provides for a National Commission for Scheduled Castes and Scheduled Tribes.

***The Constitution (66th* Amendment) Act, 1990**—The Act added State enactments relating to land reforms to the Ninth Schedule.

The Constitution (67th Amendment) Act, 1990—The Act extended President's rule in Punjab for another six months *i.e.*, total period of four years.

The Constitution (68th Amendment) Act, 1991—This Act extended President's rule in Punjab for another one years *i.e.*, total period of five years.

The Constitution (69th Amendment) Act, 1991—U.N. Territory Delhi to have 70 member Assembly and 7 member Council of Ministers to be appointed by the President. Passed by the Parliament in Dec. 1991.

The Constitution (70th Amendment) Act, 1992—This Act accorded the right to vote to the members of Pondicherry Assembly and proposed legislative Assembly for Delhi in the election of the President.

The Constitution (71th Amendment) Act, 1992—Nepali, Manipuri and Konkani added to the list of recognised languages of India. Bill was passed by the parliament in July-Aug. 1992.

The Constitution (72th Amendment) Act, 1992—For restoring peace and harmony in the areas of the state of Tripura where disturbed conditions prevailed, a memorandum of settlement was signed by the Government of India with Tripura National Volunteers.

State Election Commission

1.	State Election Commission	State Election Commissioner
2.	Appointed by	The Governor of the State
3.	Tenure	Upto the age of 62 years
4.	Status	High Court Judge
5.	Duties	To supervise, direct, and control electoral process. Preparation of electoral rolls to conduct elections to Local Bodies in the State

The Constitution (73rd Amendment) Act, 1992—This is related with Panchayati Raj.

The Constitution (74th Amendment) Act, 1992—Provided for constitutional sanctity to municipalitiess by inserting Part IX-A, containing Arts. 243P to 243 ZG and the XIIth schedule which deals with the items concerning muncipalities.

The Constitution (77th Amendment) Act, 1993—It empowers to establish tribunals to decide cases between the house owner and the person to whom the house has been given on rent.

The Constitution (78th Amendment) Act, 1995—Article 31B of the Constitution confers on the enactments included in the Ninth Schedule to the Constitution immunity from legal challenge on the ground that they violate the fundamental rights enshrined in Part III of the Constitution.

The Constitution (79th Amendment Act) 1999—It extends reservation to SCs and STs in Lok Sabha and State Legislative Assemblies for ten years beyond 2000.

The Eightieth Amendment Act, 2000—It relates to the revenue sharing between the Centre and the States whereby States' overall share was increased to 29% as per the Tenth Finance Commission's recommendation.

The Eighty First Amendment Act, 2000—It relates to carrying forward backlog vacancies of Scheduled Castes and Scheduled Tribes.

The Eighty Second Amendment Act, 2000—It relates to relaxation in qualifying marks and reservation of posts in super speciality courses in Medical and Engineering disciplines etc. for Scheduled Castes/Tribes.

The Eighty Third Amendment Act, 2001—It exempts Arunachal Pradesh from reserving seats for scheduled castes in Panchayati Raj institutions as there is no scheduled caste in Arunachal Pradesh.

The Eighty Fourth Amendment Act, 2002—The Act amended provisos to articles 82 and 170 (3) of the constitution to readjust and rationalise the territorial constituencies in the states.

The Eighty Fifth Amendment Act, 2001—It provides for the benefit of reservation in promotions in government service to the members of Scheduled Castes/Tribes.

The Eighty Sixth Amendment Act, 2002—It makes the constitutional obligation of the state to provide free elementary education to children in the 6–14 age group.

The 87th Amendment Act 2003—It substitutes the figure '2001' for the figures' 1991 in articles 81,82,170 and 330.

The 88th Amendment Act 2003—It makes minor amendments in articles 268,269 and 270 and in the seventh schedule of the constitution in List-1 Union List, after entry 92B, the following entry shall be inserted, namely.

"92 C. Taxes on Services."

The 89th Amendment Act, 2003—It amends article 338 and inserts new article 338A thereby providing for separate National Commissions for Scheduled Castes and Scheduled Tribes.

The 90th Amendment Act, 2003—It amends article 332 and inserts a new proviso about the representation of constituencies included in Bodoland Territorial Areas District in the Assam Assembly.

The Ninety First Amendment Act, 2003—It limits the size of the Council of Ministers to 15 per cent of the Lok Sabha and the Vidhan Sabhas. Also it amends the anti-defection amendment Act (52nd), 1985, debarring the defectors from holding any office of profit for the rest of the duration of the concerned legislatures.

The 92nd Amendment Act, 2003—It adds Maithili, Dogri, Bodo and Santhali in the list of languages in the eighth Schedule of the constitution raising the number of languages to 22.

93rd Constitution (Amendment) Act, 2005—It seeks to provide reservation for admission to candidates belonging to scheduled castes/tribes and other backward classes in the unaided private institutions.

The Constitution 94th (Amendment) Act, 2006—The legislation excludes Bihar from the provision of Clause (1) of Article 164 of the Constitution which provides that there shall be a Minister in charge of welfare of the Scheduled Castes and Backward classes *in Bihar, Madhya Pradesh and Orissa. It also proposes to extend the* provision of clause (1) of Article 164 to the newly formed States of Chhattisgarh and Jharkhand.

The Ninety-fifth Amendment Act, 2009—Reservation of electoral seats for SCs/STs in the Lok Sabha and State Assemblies, and nomination of Anglo-Indians in them extended for ten years from Jan. 26, 2010.

The Ninety-sixth Amendment Act, 2011—The word 'Oriya' substitued by the word 'Odia'.

The Ninety-seventh Amendment Act, 2011—Added the words "Or Co-operative Societies" after the word "Or Unions" in Article 19(1) (C) and insertion of Article 43 B *i.e.,* promotion of Co-operative Societies and added Part IX B *i.e.,* THE CO-OPERATIVE SOCIETIES. The 98th Amendment Act, 2013 Added Article 371 (J) in the Constitution.

The Ninety-Eight Amendment Act, 2012—To empower the Governor of Karnataka to take step to develop Hyderabad Karnataka region.

The Ninety-Ninth Amendment Act, 2014—Insertion of new articles 124A, 124B, 124C, Amendments to articles 127, 128, 217, 222, 224A, 231.

The Hundredth Amendment Act, 2015—Amendment to first Schedule to Constitution.

101st Amendment Act, 2016—GST Passed.

102nd Amendment Act, 2018—Constitutional Status to National Commission for Backward Classes.

103rd Amendment Act, 2019—A maximum of 10% reservation for economically weaker sections of classes other than the classes mentioned in clauses (4) and (5) of Article 15, *i.e.,* classes other than socially and economically backward classes of citizens for the SC and the ST.

104th Amendment Act, 2019—To extend the reservation of seats of SCs and STs in the Lok Sabha and states assemblies from Seventy years to Eighty years. Removed the reserved seats for the Anglo-Indian community in the Lok Sabha and state assemblies.

105th Amendment Act, 2021—State Government retores the power of Identifying and Specifying their own OBC Lists.

106th Amendment Act, 2023—To reserve one-third of the seats in the Lok Sabha (330A), State Legislative Assemblies (332A) and Delhi Legislative Assembly (239AA) for women for a period for 15 years after coming into effect (334A).

Schedules of the Constitution

1.	First Schedule	List of States and Union Territories
2.	Second Schedule	Remuneration and emoluments to Constitutional Authorities
3.	Third Schedule	Forms of Oaths and Affirmations
4.	Fourth Schedule	Allocation of Seats in Rajya Sabha
5.	Fifth Schedule	Administration of Scheduled areas
6.	Sixth Schedule	Administration of Tribal areas
7.	Seventh Schedule	List of Subjects, Central, States and Concurrent.
8.	Eighth Schedule	List of National Languages
9.	Ninth Schedule	Acts and orders, relating to land reforms
10.	Tenth Schedule	Anti-defection Act
11.	Eleventh Schedule	Panchayat Raj system
12.	Twelfth Schedule	3 types of Municipalities (Urban Local Self Government)

News Agencies

Indian News Agencies—There are Five News Agencies in India—

(1) The Press Trust of India;

(2) The United News of India; Khabar (Urdu);

(3) Samachar Bharati;

(4) Hindustan Samachar;

(5) Bhasha.

P.T.I. and U.N.I. serve the media through English news whereas the Samachar Bharati, Hindustan Samachar Kendra and Bhasha service through various Languages of India. U.N.I. started an Urdu News Agency 'Khabar'.

Foreign News Agencies—(1) The Reuters of the United Kingdom, (2) Agency France Press of France, (3) Associated Press, (4) United Press of America, (5) International News Services of the United States, (6) Tass of the Soviet Union, (7) Globe (Near and Far East Agency), (8) Arab News Agency, (9) N.C.N.A. (China), (10) Cetaka (Czechoslovakia), (11) Antara (Indonesia), (12) Kyodo (Japan), (13) Novosty Press Agency (U.S.S.R.), (14) Bangladesh Sangbad Sangastha, Dhaka (Bangladesh), (15) Iraq News Agency (INA)—Iraq.

Railways

Indian Railway has grown into Asia's largest and the World's Fourth largest railway system under a single management. Presently (As on August 2024) it is a single system which consists of 68,584 route km of track that criss-cross the country, on which more than 22 thousand number of trains per day, carrying about 2·40 crore passengers and hauling nearly 3·3 million tonnes of freight everyday.

Indian Railways till March 2024 consisted of 4,397 diesel and 10,675 electric locomotives. Hence, the total number of locomotives in Indian Railways till March 2024 was 15,110 and 7,461 stations.

Technical

Route km—69,181 km

(i) Broad Gauge (1676 mm)—66,820 km

(ii) Meter Gauge (1000 mm)—1159 km

(iii) Narrow Gauge (762 mm & 610 mm)—1202 km

Track length—1,09,748 km

Electrification—*62,253 km*

Indian Railways employs around 1·3 million people.

Railway Zones (with Headquarters)

The 19 zones and their respective headquarters are given below :

	Zonal Railway	Headquarters
1.	Central Railway	Mumbai CST
2.	Eastern Railway	Kolkata
3.	Northern Railway	New Delhi
4.	North Eastern Railway	Gorakhpur
5.	North-East Frontier Railway	Maligaon (Guwahati)
6.	Southern Railway	Chennai
7.	South Central Railway	Secunderabad
8.	South Eastern Railway	Kolkata
9.	Western Railway	Church Gate, Mumbai
10.	East Central Railway	Hajipur
11.	East Coast Railway	Bhubaneshwar
12.	North Central Railway	Prayagraj
13.	North Western Railway	Jaipur
14.	South East Central Railway	Bilaspur
15.	South Western Railway	Hubli
16.	West Central Railway	Jabalpur
17.	Kolkata Metro Railway	Kolkata
18.	South Coast Railway	Visakhapatnam
19.	Konkan Railway	Navi Mumbai

Headquarters of the Railway Service Commission—Mumbai, Kolkata, Allahabad, Chennai, Bhopal, Ahmedabad, Ajmer, Bangalore, Bhubaneshwar, Bilaspur, Chandigarh, Gorakhpur, Guwahati, Jammu, Malda, Muzaffarpur, Patna, Ranchi, Secunderabad, Siliguri and Thiruvananthapuram.

Railway Staff College—Baroda.

Important Long Distance Trains

	Name of the Train	Runs between	Distance (in km)
1.	Vivek Express (India's longest)	Dibrugarh-Kanya Kumari (Weekly)	4,279
2.	Himsagar Express	Jammu-Kanyakumari (Weekly)	3,726
3.	Guwahati-Trivandrum Express	Guwahati-Trivandrum	3,574
4.	Kochin-Guwahati Express	Kochin-Guwahati (Weekly)	3,362
5.	Kerala Express	New Delhi-Trivandrum	3,054
6.	Gorakhpur-Cochin Express	Gorakhpur-Cochin Harbour (Bi-Weekly)	2,991
7.	Rajkot-Trivandrum Express	Rajkot-Trivandrum (Weekly)	2,734
8.	Karnataka Express	New Delhi Bengaluru	2,444
9.	Grand Trunk Express	New Delhi-Chennai	2,190
10.	Tamil Nadu Express	New Delhi-Chennai (4 days a week)	2,190

British Provinces

S. No.	Name	H.Q.
1.	Assam	Shillong
2.	Baluchistan	Quetta
3.	Bengal Presidency	Calcutta
4.	Bihar (Bifurcated from Bengal 1912)	Patna
5.	Bombay Presidency	Bombay
6.	Central Province	Nagpur
7.	Delhi (From 1912)	New Delhi
8.	Madras Presidency	Madras
9.	North West Frontier (1932 - became province)	Peshawar
10.	Orissa (Bifurcated from Bihar in 1935)	Cuttack
11.	Punjab	Lahore
12.	Sind	Hyderabad
13.	United Provinces	Lucknow

British Provinces - 1947
(Bifurcated from India)

	Name	H.Q.
	PAKISTAN – 1947	**KARACHI**
1.	Baluchistan	Quetta
2.	N. W. Frontier	Peshawar
3.	Punjab (West)	Lahore
4.	Sind	Hyderabad
5.	Bengal (East)	Dhaka
6.	14 Princely States acceded to Pakistan.	
	Total Area	8,03,943 Sq. km.
	BANGLADESH - 1971	DHAKA
1.	East Bengal after liberation from Pakistan	Dhaka
	Total Area	1,44,020 Sq. km

Indian Provinces - 1947
(After bifurcation)

S. No.	'A' States	H.Q.
1.	Assam	Shillong
2.	Bengal (West)	Calcutta
3.	Bihar	Patna
4.	Bombay	Bombay
5.	Central Province	Nagpur
6.	Madras	Madras
7.	Orissa	Cuttack
8.	Punjab (East)	Chandigarh
9.	United Province (Uttar Pradesh)	Lucknow
'B'	***States and territories***	
	562 Princely States amalgamated into Indian Union	Formed as 26 of 'B' States and territories

Neighbouring Countries

1.	North	China, Nepal, Bhutan
2.	North-West	Afghanistan and Pakistan
3.	West	Pakistan
4.	East	Bangladesh, Myanmar
5.	South	Sri Lanka

On 15th August, 1947

"Long years ago we made a tryst with destiny and now the time comes when we shall redeem our pledge, not wholly or in full measure, but very substantially. At the stroke of midnight hour, when the world sleeps, India will awake to life and freedom."

— Jawaharlal Nehru

Independent India (Dominion Status) 15.8.1947 to 25.1.1950

1.	Governor-General (Appointed by King of United Kingdom)	1. Lord Mountbatten (15.8.1947 to 20.6.1948) 2. C. Rajagopalachari (21.6.1948 to 25.1.1950)
2.	Prime Minister	Jawaharlal Nehru
3.	Speaker, Parliament	G. V. Mavlankar
4.	Chief Justice, Federal Court	Justice H. R. Kania

First Indian Cabinet (15.8.1947)

S.No.	Name of the Minister	Portfolio
1.	Jawaharlal Nehru	Prime Minister, External Affairs and Commonwealth Affairs.
2.	Sardar Vallabh Bhai Patel	Deputy Prime Minister, Home, States and Information and Broadcasting
3.	Dr. Rajendra Prasad	Food and Agriculture
4.	Maulana Abul Kalaam Azad	Education
5.	John Mathai	Railways and Transport
6.	Jagjivan Ram	Labour
7.	C. H. Babha	Commerce
8.	Rafi Ahmed Kidwai	Communications
9.	Sardar Baldev Singh	Defence
10.	Rajkumari Amrit Kaur	Health
11.	Dr. B. R. Ambedkar	Law
12.	R. K. Shanmugam Chetty	Finance
13.	S. P. Mukerjee	Industry and Supply
14.	N. V. Gadgil	Works, Mines, Power

National Holidays and Indian Standard Time

1. National Holidays

1. Republic Day (26th January)
2. Independence Day (15th August)
3. Gandhi Jayanti (2nd October)

2. Indian Standard Time

It is fixed on the mean time of $82\frac{1}{2}°$ (E) meridian which passes through near Mirzapur (UP).

(5 Hrs and 30 Mts of Greenwich Time ahead)

Greenwich Mean Time

It is based on the local time of the meridian passing through Greenwich near London (It is the standard time of U.K.).

Local Time for any place

It varies from the Greenwich time at the rate of 4 minutes for each degree of Longitude.

INDIAN ARMED FORCE

Chief of Defence Staff (CDS)

Chief of Defence Staff (CDS) is the professional service chief, head of the Indian Armed Forces and the senior-most uniformed military adviser to the Government of India. The position was first officially suggested in 1999 following the Kargil War through the recommendations of the Kargil Review Committee. Although a long-talked-about position in India, the official call was made public by Prime Minister Narendra Modi during his Independence Day speech on 15 August, 2019 at Red Fort, New Delhi. On 24 December, 2019, the Cabinet Committee on Security (CCS) formally announced the creation of the position, a four-star general, a tri-service chief, that shall lead the defence forces as well as take up other roles such as the secretary of the Department of Military Affairs under the Ministry of Defence.

It is considered that the Chief of Defence Staff is a critical position in today's era of hybrid warfare, and will help increase jointmanship, tri-service effectiveness and overall combat capabilities of India. It is speculated that the civil service Defence Secretary will be the main 'defence' advisor, whilst the CDS will assume the role of being the main 'military' advisory, acting as the single-point military advisor to the government and Prime Minister. India was the only large democracy which did not have a single point military advisor; with all P5 countries having one.

General Bipin Rawat took over as the first CDS on 1st January, 2020. Gen. Rawat died in a helicopter crash in Kannur (Tamil Nadu) on December 8, 2021

Present Chief of Defence Staff (CDS)—Anil Chauhan (Feb. 2025)

Army

The Chief is 'Chief of the Army Staff'. Its headquarters is in New Delhi. The army is organised into the following seven commands :

1. Central Command	Lucknow (Uttar Pradesh)
2. Eastern Command	Kolkata (West Bengal)
3. Northern Command	Udhampur (Jammu & Kashmir)
4. Southern Command	Pune (Maharashtra)
5. South-West Command	Jaipur (Rajasthan)
6. Western Command	Chandimandir, Panchkula (Haryana)
7. Training Command (ARTRAC)	Shimla (Himachal Pradesh)

Air Force

The Chief is an Air Chief Marshal ranked 'Chief of the Air Staff'. Its headquarters is in New Delhi. The Air force is organized into seven commands :

1. Central Air Command	Allahabad (Uttar Pradesh)
2. Eastern Air Command	Shillong (Meghalaya)
3. Southern Air Command	Thiruvananthapuram (Kerala)
4. South-Western Air Command	Gandhi Nagar (Gujarat)
5. Western Air Command	New Delhi (New Delhi)
6. Training Command	Bengaluru (Karnataka)
7. Maintenance Command	Nagpur (Maharashtra)

Navy

The Chief is an Admiral ranked 'Chief of the Naval Staff'. The headquarters is in New Delhi. The Navy has three Naval Commands :

1. Western Naval Command	Mumbai (Maharashtra)
2. Eastern Naval Command	Visakhapatnam (Andhra Pradesh)
3. Southern Naval Command	Kochi (Kerala)

Commissioned Ranks

Army	Air Force	Navy
● General	Air Chief Marshal	Admiral
● Lieutenant General	Air Marshal	Vice-Admiral
● Major General	Air Vice-Marshal	Rear Admiral
● Brigadier	Air Commodore	Commodore
● Colonel	Group Captain	Captain
● Lieutenant Colonel	Wing Commander	Colonel Commander
● Major	Squadron Leader	Lieutenant Commander
● Captain	Flight Lieutenant	Lieutenant
● Lieutenant	Flying Officer	Sub Lieutenant

Indian Defence Training Institutions

Army (Institution)	Place
● National Defence Academy (NDA)	Khadakwasla (Pune)
● National Defence College (NDC)	New Delhi
● College of Defence Management (CDM)	Secunderabad (Telangana)
● College of Military Engineering (CME)	Pune (Maharashtra)
● Rashtriya Indian Military College (RIMC)	Dehradun (Founded on 13 March, 1922)
● Indian Military Academy (IMA)	Dehradun (Uttarakhand)
● Armed Forces Medical College (AFMC)	Pune
● Officer's Training Academy (OTA)	Chennai, (Tamil Nadu) and Gaya (Bihar)
● High Altitude Warfare Schoool	Gulmarg (J & K)
● Counter Insurgency and Jungle Warfare School	Vairengte (Mizoram)
● Infantry Schools	Mhow and Belgaum
● Armoured Corps Centre and School	Ahmednagar (Maharashtra)
● School of Artillery	Devlali

Air Force (Institution)	Place
● Air Force School	Sambra (Belgaum)
● Flying Instructors School	Tambaram
● Helicopter Training School	Avadi
● College of Air Warfare	Secunderabad
● Air Force Administrative College	Coimbatore
● Air Force Academy	Hyderabad
● Air Force Technical College	Jalahalli (Bengaluru)
● Elementary Flying School	Bidar
● Paratroopers Training School	Agra (UP)
● Institute of Aerospace Medicine	Bengaluru

Navy (Institution)	Place
● I.N.S. Chilka	Bhubaneswar (Odisha)
● I.N.S. Hansa	Goa
● *Navy Shipwright School*	*Visakhapatnam*
● I.N.S. Satavahana	Visakhapatnam (A. P.)
● I.N.S. Garuda	Kochi (Cochin)

● I.N.S. Shivaji	Lonavala
● I.N.S. Valsura	Jamnagar (Gujarat)
● I.N.S. Hamla	Mumbai
● I.N.S. Kunjali	Mumbai
● I.N.S. Ashwini (INM)	Mumbai
● I.N.S. Agrani	Coimbatore
● Naval Academy	Goa

Internal Security of India

Organization	Year	Headquarter
● Assam Rifles (AR) (Former Cachar Levy)	1835	Shillong
● Central Reserve Police Force (CRPF)	1939	New Delhi
● National Cadet Corps (NCC)	1948	New Delhi
● Territorial Army (TA)	1949	In different states
● Indo-Tibetan Border Police (ITBP)	1962	New Delhi
● Home Guards (HG)	1962	In different states
● Border Security Force (BSF)	1965	New Delhi
● Central Industrial Security Force (CISF)	1969	New Delhi
● Indian Coast Guards (CG)	1977	New Delhi
● National Security Guards (NSG)	1984	New Delhi

Crop Seasons

1. Rabi crops	Sown in October, November
Wheat, Grams, Linseed, Mustard, Pulses, Barley etc.	
2. Kharif Crops	Sown in June
Rice, Millets, Maize, Cotton, Groundnuts Jute etc.	
3. Zaid Crops	Sown in March to June
Watermelon, Muskmelon, Cucumber, Vegetable etc.	

CHRONOLOGICAL HIGHLIGHTS

1. October 1949	Territorial Army raised.
2. October 26, 1962	President promulgates the Defence of India Ordinance.
3. August 14, 1963	NCC training made compulsory.
4. July 2, 1972	Simla Agreement signed between India and Pakistan.
5. May 18, 1974	India's first underground Nuclear Blast.
6. May 21, 1989	Successful launch of 'AGNI' at Chandipur, Orissa.
7. June 5, 1989	'Trishul' - India's surface-to-surface missile successfully test-fired.

8. March 1, 1993	'Arjun' - India's main battle tank launched.
9. May 11, 1998	India conducts three underground Nuclear Tests.
10. May 13, 1998	India conducts two more underground Nuclear Tests.
11. January 4, 2001	Indigenously developed Light Combat Aircraft (LCA) successfully test flown.
12. Feb. 12, 2003	India's Supersonic missile **BrahMos**, built with Russian collaboration, was successfully test-fired.
13. April 18, 2003	India's first indigenous stealth frigate **INS Shivalik** was launched at Muzagaon Docks.
14. May 4, 2003	India's Light Combat Aircraft (LCA) named 'Tejas' (radiance) by the Prime Minister Mr. A. B. Vajpayee.
15. Aug. 1, 2003	L.C.A. goes supersonic.
16. Oct. 9, 2003	Indian Naval Fast Attack Craft-T82 (INFAC-T82) inducted into the Indian Navy.
17. June 4, 2004	India's second indigenous stealth warship **INS Satpura**, second of the P-17 frigate series launched at the Mazagaon Docks in Mumbai.
18. June 13, 2004	India-Russia jointly developed surface to surface missile 'BrahMos' test fired from test centre situated in Chandipur, Orissa.
19. Nov. 28, 2004	The first indigenously built multi-role Sukhoi MKI fighter aircraft manufactured at HAL was inducted in Indian Air Force.
20. Dec. 21, 2004	The Indo-Russian supersonic cruise missile **Brah-Mos** was test fired for the first time in a 'land-to-land role' in Pokhran (Rajasthan).
21. April 15, 2005	The new South Western Command of Indian Army established in Jaipur (Raj.) making it the 7th Command of Indian Army.
22. June, 2007	I.N.S. Jalashwa joins the Eastern Command of the Indian Navy. It has been acquired from the USA which had commissioned it in the US Navy by the name of USS Trenton. It is the second warship included in the Indian Navy after I.N.S. Virat.
23. May 2009	The flight trial of Astra missile was carried out by scientists of the DRDO of Balasore, Orissa.
24. April 12, 2007	India successfully tested its home-grown nuclear capable Agni-III ballistic missile with a range of over 3000 km from Balasore, Orissa.
25. Feb. 26, 2008	Sagarika Missile Test fired successfully.
26. June 20, 2008	'Nishant' India's unmanned Aerial Vehicle developed by DRDO, was successfully flight tested near Kolar.
27. Nov. 20, 2009	Two women, Sub Lieutenants Seema Rani Sharma and Ambica Hooda, commissioned into the Indian Navy, became the first combatants in the armed forces.
28. August 2010	Russia hands over Akula N. Submarine to India.
29. 2011	SFC successfully performs a test of the Nuclear capable solid fueled AGN-1 ballistic Missile.
30. 2012	*First indigenous* radar imaging satellite launched.
31. 2013	Mars orbiter mission launched on Nov. 5.
32. 2014	GSLV-D-5 successfully launched GSAT-14 from Shriharikota.

33. 2015 ASTROSAT. India's first dedicated multi wavelength space observatory launched.

34. 2016 IRNSS-1E launched on 20 Jan., 2016

35. 2016 IRNSS-1G launched on 28 April, 2016.

36. 2017 Communication Satellite GSAT-17 launched on June 29, 2017.

37. 2018 Navigation and Global Positioning Satellite IRNSS-1I launched on April 12, 2018 from Sriharikota.

Communication Satellite GSAT-29 launched on Nov. 15, 2018 from Sriharikota.

38. 2020 The Rudram-project previously referred as DRDO Anti-Radiation Missile (ARM) or new generation anti-radiation missile (NGARM) is an air-to-surface anti-radiation missile in development by the Defence Research and Development Organisation of India, launched from a Sukhoi-30 MKI on 11 October, 2020.

39. 2021 Sindhunetra Satellite deployed in space on February 28, 2021; Indian Navy gets INS Visakhapatnam on Nov. 21, 2021.

40. 2022 ISRO successfully conducted the qualification test of cryogenic Engine for Gaganyaan programme, Mahendragiri, Tamil Nadu on 12 Jan., 2022, India successfully test-fired and advanced sea to sea variant of BrahMOS on 20 Jan., DRDO successfully flight tested the final deliverable configuration of the man portable Anti-Tank Guided Missile on 11 Jan., The PSLV-C52 is the 54th mission of the Indian Polar Satellite Launch Vehicle (PSLV) program. PSLV-C52 was launched with the RISAT-IA (EOS-04), INSPIRE Sat, INS-2TD as its main payload on 14 February, Europe's Arianespace launches India's GSAT-24 (23 June), ISRO's PSLV-C53 launches 3 Singapore Satellites (30 June), ISRO successfuly launched 36 satellites on a mission called LVM3-M2 (23 Oct.), ISRO successfully launches PSLV-C54 carrying 9 satellites *viz.*, oceansat-3 and 8 Nano satellites (26 Nov.).

41. 2023 On January 3, 2023, EOS SAT-1, the initial satellite of EOSSAT, the first agri-focused satellite constellation launched by a remote sensing company, was successfully delivered into a low Earth Orbit by Space X's Falcon 9 rocket from the Cape Canveral Space Force Station in Florida.

Chandrayaan-3—Chandrayaan-3 was launched on 14 July, 2023, at 2 : 35 pm IST as scheduled, from Satish Dhawan Space Centre Second Launch Pad in Sriharikota, Andhra Pradesh. India has made history as it became the first country to land (Vikram lander) on the South Pole of the lunar surface on 23rd August, 2023.

42. 2024 On January 10, 2024, India unveils new indegenous assault rifle 'Ugram' for Armed Forces, first survey vessel Large INS Sandhayak commissioned on 10 Feb., 2024, Rudra M-11 Missile test-fires successfully off Odisha coast on May 30, 2024.

ISRO Announces Indo-French Satellite Mission TRISHNA (5 June), Three Craters Discovered on Mars by Scientists of Physical Research Laboratory (12 June); ISRO launches Earth Observation Satellite EOS-08 (16 Aug.); Bharatiya Antriksh Station (BAS) our own space station for scientific research to be established with the launch of its first module in 2028 (18 Sept.)

43. 2025 **GSLV**—F 15 is the 17th flight of India's Geosynchronous satellite launched Vehicle (GSLV) on 29 January, 2025.

Hill Stations

1.	Almora, Mussoorie, Nainital	Uttarakhand
2.	Cherrapunji (Shillong), Khasi Hills (Shillong)	Meghalaya
3.	Ooty, Kodaikanal, Yercaud	Tamil Nadu
4.	Dalhousie, Kassauli (Shimla)	Himachal Pradesh
5.	Darjeeling	West Bengal
6.	Gulmarg, Srinagar	Jammu & Kashmir
7.	Mahabaleshwar	Maharashtra
8.	Mt. Abu	Rajasthan
9.	Pachmarhi	Madhya Pradesh
10.	Hazaribagh	Jharkhand
11.	Pahalgam	Jammu and Kashmir
12.	Shillong	Meghalaya

National Parks

1.	Corbett National Park	Nainital, Uttarakhand
2.	Dudhwa National Park	Lakhimpur Kheri, Uttar Pradesh
3.	Kaziranga National Park	Jorhat, Assam
4.	Kanha National Park	Jabalpur, Bhedaghat, Madhya Pradesh
5.	Gir National Park	Rajkot, Junagadh, Gujarat
6.	Guindy National Park	Guindy, Chennai, Tamil Nadu
7.	Nagarhole National Park	Coorg, Karnataka
8.	Bandipur National Park	Mysore, Karnataka
9.	Periyar National Park	Kerala
10.	Ranthambore National Park	Rajasthan

National Wildlife Sanctuaries

1.	Dachigam Wildlife Sanctuary	Srinagar, Jammu & Kashmir
2.	Sariska	Alwar, Rajasthan
3.	Hazaribagh Wildlife Sanctuary	Hazaribagh, Jharkhand
4.	Ranthambore National Park (Tiger Project)	Sawai Madhopur, Rajasthan
5.	Mudhumalai Wildlife Sanctuary	Mudumalai, Nilgiris, Tamil Nadu
6.	Periyar Wildlife Sanctuary	Idukki, Kottayam, Kerala
7.	National Chambal (Gharial) wildlife Sanctuary	Etawah, Uttar Pradesh

Holy Places in India

1.	Amarnath	Kashmir
2.	Ayodhya	*Uttar Pradesh*
3.	*Badrinath*	Uttarakhand
4.	Dwaraka	Gujarat

5.	Haridwar	Uttarakhand
6.	Kancheepuram	Tamil Nadu
7.	Kedarnath	Uttarakhand
8.	Mathura	Uttar Pradesh
9.	Puri	Odisha
10.	Rameswaram	Tamil Nadu
11.	Tirupati	Andhra Pradesh
12.	Ujjain	Madhya Pradesh
13.	Varanasi	Uttar Pradesh

Scientific and Industrial Research

1.	Department of Scientific and Industrial Research	To encourage industries to use available infrastructure for R & D requirements
2.	National Research Development Corporation	Technological transfer organisation, commercialise indigenously developed technology (low cost heart valve)
3.	Central Electronics Limited	Photo Voltare through research and development
4.	Council of Scientific and Industrial Research	With network of laboratories spearhead in basic and applied science

Civil Aviation

(National Airport Authority 1986)

At present (January 2023) the Authority manages 137 airports including 34 international, 10 customs airports, 103 domestic airports and 23 civil enclaves of defence air fields. Some important AAI airports are given below—

1. Agartala (Agartala Airport)
2. Ahmedabad (Sardar Vallabhbhai Patel International Airport)
3. Aizawl (Lengpui Airport)
4. Belgaum (Belgaum Airport)
5. Bengaluru (Bengaluru International Airport)
6. Bhopal (Raja Bhoj Airport)
7. Anna Meenambkkam, Chennai (Chennai International Airport)
8. Dibrugarh (Dibrugarh Airport)
9. Dimapur (Dimapur Airport)

10. Dehradun (Jolly Grant Airport)
11. Gwalior (Gwalior Airport)
12. Guwahati (Lokpriya Gopinath Bordoloi International Airport)
13. Goa (Mopa—Manohar International Airport)
14. Hyderabad (Rajiv Gandhi International Airport)
15. Imphal (Tulihal Airport)
16. Jaipur (Jaipur International Airport)
17. Jammu (Jammu Airport)
18. Jamshedpur (Sonari Airport)
19. Jabalpur (Jabalpur Airport)
20. Jalgaon (Jalgaon Airport)
21. Kochi (Cochin International Airport)
22. Kozhikode (Calicut International Airport)
23. Kolkata (Netaji Subhash Chandra Bose International Airport)
24. Khajuraho (Khajuraho Airport)
25. Lucknow Chaudhary Charan Singh (Amausi International Airport)
26. Madurai (Madurai Airport)
27. Mumbai (Chhatrapati Shivaji International Airport)
28. New Delhi (Indira Gandhi International Airport)
29. Nagpur (Dr. Babasaheb Ambedkar International Airport)
30. Pune (Pune Airport)
31. Patna (Lok Nayak Jayaprakash International Airport)
32. Raipur (Swami Vivekananda Airport)
33. Ranchi (Birsa Munda Airport)
34. Shillong (Zaruki International Airport)
35. Surat (Surat Airport)
36. Shimla (Shimla Airport)
37. Salem (Salem Airport)
38. Tiruchirappalli (Tiruchirapalli International Airport)
39. Varanasi (Lal Bahadur Shastri International Airport)
40. Itanagar (Donyi Polo Airport).

Life Insurance Corporation of India

1. Nationalised on	1.9.1956
(a) Insurance Companies Indian and Foreign Companies	245
(b) Central office	Mumbai
(c) Zonal office	Mumbai, Kolkata, Delhi, Chennai, Hyderabad, Kanpur, Bhopal, Patna
(d) Divisional offices	113
(e) Branch offices	2048
2. General Insurance Company Nationalised on —	22 November, 1972
(a) Subsidiary Companies Total units	107 (groups - 4)
National Insurance Company Ltd.	Kolkata
New India Assurance Co. Ltd.	Mumbai
Oriental Insurance Co. Ltd.	New Delhi
United India Insurance Co. Ltd.	Chennai

Major Ports

I. Western Zone

1. Mumbai (Largest)
2. (Deendayal Port) Kandla (1957)
3. Mormugao (1963)
4. New Mangalore (1974)
5. Cochin
6. Jawaharlal Nehru Port, Mumbai (1989)
7. Port Blair (June 1, 2010)

II. Eastern Zone

1. Chennai
2. Vishakhapatnam (Largest National Port)
3. Kolkata-Haldia (1977)
4. Paradeep (1966)
5. V.O. Chidambaram Tuticorin (1974)
6. Kamaraj Port, Ennore (1999)

Postal Services

1. Postal Services commenced	1837
(a) First postage stamp issued at Karachi	1852
2. Separate Postal Dept. commenced	1854
(a) No. of Post offices	700
(b) M.O. introduced	1880
(c) Savings Bank Service	1882
(d) Postal Life Insurance	1884
3. Postal Mail Service	1907
4. Air Mail Service	1911
5. Posts & Telecommunication started	1984
Total Post Offices (2023-24)	1,64,972
Quick Mail Service	1975
Speed Post	1986
E-Post	2002

Important Days and Dates

Dates	Days
1 January	World Peace Day
12 January	National Youth Day
2 February	World Wetlands Day
28 February	National Science Day
3 March	World Wildlife Day
22 March	World Water Day
22 April	World Earth Day
5 June	World Environment Day
11 July	World Population Day
29 August	National Sports Day
16 September	World Ozone Day
12 October	World Arthritis Day
16 October	World Food Day
14 November	Jawaharlal Nehru's Birthday
1 December	World Aids Day
18 December	World Migrants Day

National Bank

Nationalized Bank in India

S.N.	Anchor Bank		Estd.
1.	State Bank of India	–	1955
2.	Bank of India	–	1906
3.	Bank of Maharashtra	–	1935
4.	Canara Bank	–	1906
5.	Central Bank of India	–	1911
6.	Indian Bank	–	1907
7.	Indian Overseas Bank	–	1937
8.	Punjab and Sind Bank	–	1908
9.	Punjab National Bank	–	1894
10.	Bank of Baroda	–	1908
11.	UCO Bank	–	1943
12.	Union Bank of India	–	1919

Stock Exchanges

1. *Mumbai*
2. *Chennai*
3. Coimbatore
4. Kolkata
5. New Delhi
6. Ahmedabad
7. Vadodara
8. Rajkot
9. Kutch

10. Hyderabad	11. Bengaluru	12. Mangalore
13. Hubli-Dharwar	14. Kochi	15. Bhubaneshwar
16. Jaipur	17. Indore	18. Kanpur
19. Ludhiana	20. Guwahati	21. Magadh (Patna)

All India Services

1. Indian Administrative Service
2. Indian Audit and Accounts Service
3. Indian Foreign Service
4. Indian Forest Service
5. Indian Police Service
6. Indian Postal Service
7. Indian Revenue Service

Agricultural Products and their Chief Producing States (2023-24)

Product	Chief Producers in terms of Yield
1. Barley	(1) Rajasthan; (2) Uttar Pradesh; (3) Haryana
2. Rice	(1) Telangana; (2) Uttar Pradesh; (3) West Bengal
3. Wheat	(1) Uttar Pradesh; (2) Madhya Pradesh; (3) Punjab
4. Bajara	(1) Rajasthan; (2) Uttar Pradesh; (3) Gujarat
5. Maize	(1) Karnataka; (2) Bihar; (3) Madhya Pradesh
6. Tur	(1) Karnataka; (2) Maharashtra; (3) Uttar Pradesh
7. Gram	(1) Madhya Pradesh; (2) Maharashtra; (3) Rajasthan
8. Urad	(1) Madhya Pradesh; (2) Uttar Pradesh; (3) Andhra Pradesh
9. Moong	(1) Madhya Pradesh; (2) Rajasthan; (3) Bihar
10. Lentil	(1) Madhya Pradesh; (2) Uttar Pradesh; (3) West Bengal
11. Ground-nut	(1) Gujarat; (2) Rajasthan; (3) Madhya Pradesh
12. Soyabean	(1) Madhya Pradesh; (2) Maharashtra; (3) Rajasthan
13. Sugar-cane	(1) Uttar Pradesh; (2) Maharashtra; (3) Karnataka
14. Cotton	(1) Gujarat; (2) Maharashtra; (3) Telangana
15. Jute	(1) West Bengal; (2) Bihar, (3) Assam

Average Temperature of Some Important Cities of the World

Name of the City	Temperature in °C July	January
1. Moscow	18·3	−9·4
2. London	18·0	4·5
3. New Delhi	31·1	13·9
4. Canberra	5·6	20·0
5. Buenos Aires	10·0	23·3
6. Ottawa	20·6	−11·1
7. Beijing	26·0	−4·4
8. Paris	18·0	3·0
9. Berlin	19·0	−0·5
10. Tokyo	24·4	3·0
11. Amsterdam	16·5	2·3
12. Islamabad	32·2	10·0
13. Brasillia	17·8	22·2
14. New York	23·3	−1·1
15. Cairo	28·3	−13·3

Principal Mountain Peaks of the World

	Mountains	Height in Metres	Range	Date of First Ascent
1.	Mount Everest	8,850	Himalayas	May 29, 1953
2.	K-2 (Godwin Austen)	8,611	Karakoram	July 31, 1954
3.	Kanchenjunga	8,597	Himalayas	May 25, 1955
4.	Lhotse	8,511	Himalayas	May 18, 1956
5.	Makalu I	8,481	Himalayas	May 15, 1955
6.	Dhaulagiri I	8,167	Himalayas	May 13, 1960
7.	Mansalu I	8,156	Himalayas	May 9, 1956
8.	Chollyo	8,153	Himalayas	Oct. 19, 1954
9.	Nanga Parbat	8,124	Himalayas	July 3, 1953
10.	Annapurna I	8,091	Himalayas	June 3, 1950
11.	Gasherbrum I	8,068	Karakoram	July 5, 1958
12.	Broad Peak I	8,047	Karakoram	June 9, 1957
13.	Gasherbrum II	8,034	Karakoram	July 7, 1956
14.	Shisha Pangma (Gosainthan)	8,014	Himalayas	May 2, 1964
15.	Gasherbrum III	7,952	Karakoram	Aug. 11, 1975

First in India

1.	British Governor General of Bengal	Warren Hastings
2.	Governor General of Independent India	Lord Mountbatten
3.	Commander-in-chief of Free India	General Roy Bucher
4.	Cosmonaut	Sqn. Ldr. Rakesh Sharma
5.	Emperor of Moghul Dynasty in India	Babar
6.	Field Marshal	S. H. F. J. Manekshaw
7.	Indian Governor General of Indian Union	C. Rajagopalachari
8.	Indian I.C.S. Officer	Satyendra Nath Tagore
9.	Indian Member of Viceroy's Executive Council	Sri S.P. Sinha
10.	Indian to swim across English Channel	Mihir Sen
11.	Indian woman to swim across English Channel	Miss Arati Saha
12.	Man to climb Mount Everest	Tenzing Norgay
13.	Man to climb Mount Everest without Oxygen	Phu Dorjee
14.	Man to climb Mount Everest twice	Nwang Gombu
15.	Nobel Prize winner	Rabindra Nath Tagore (1913)
16.	President of Indian National Congress	W. C. Banerjee
17.	President of Indian Republic	Dr. Rajendra Prasad
18.	*Talkie Film*	Alam Ara (1931)
19.	Test Tube Baby (Documented)	Indira
20.	Viceroy of India	Lord Canning

21. Woman Minister of Indian Union — Rajkumari Amrit Kaur
22. Woman Chief Minister of State — Mrs. Sucheta Kriplani
23. Woman Governor — Mrs. Sarojini Naidu
24. Woman President of Indian National Congress — Dr. Annie Besant
25. Woman Prime Minister — Mrs. Indira Gandhi
26. Woman Speaker of a State Assembly — Mrs. Shanno Devi
27. Prime Minister of India — Pt. Jawahar Lal Nehru
28. Muslim President of Indian Union — Dr. Zakir Hussain
29. Speaker of Lok Sabha — G. V. Mavlankar
30. Woman to climb mount Everest — Bachhendri Pal
31. Woman Judge in Supreme Court — Mrs. Meera Sahib Fatima Biwi
32. Woman Chief Justice of a High Court — Smt. Leela Seth
33. Indian Woman to go in space (Now U.S. Citizen) — Kalpana Chawla
34. The first Indian weightlifter to win bronze medal in Olympics — Karnam Malleshwari (Sydney, in 2000)
35. The First Indian World Chess Champion — Vishwanathan Anand
36. India's first paperless Newspaper — The News Today (Launched on Jan. 3, 2001)
37. India's First woman Merchant Navy Officer — Sonali Banerjee
38. The first Dalit Speaker of the Lok Sabha — G. M. C. Balyogi
39. The first Vice-President of India to die in harness — Krishna Kant
40. The first Indian woman cricketer to score double century — Mithali Raj (August 2002 playing against England)
41. The first woman Air Vice-Marshal — P. Bandopadhyaya
42. The first Indian to be appointed as United Nations Civilian Police Advisor — Ms. Kiran Bedi
43. The first astronaut of Indian origin to perish aboard U.S. space shuttle in a tragic accident — Dr. Kalpana Chawla (Columbia space shuttle, Feb. 1, 2003)
44. The first woman to be appointed Deputy Governor of Reserve Bank of India — K. J. Udeshi (appointed on June 10, 2003)
45. The first Indian girl to register a win in a Wimbledon tournament — Sania Mirza (2003)
46. The first Indian lady to win a medal in World Athletic Championship — Anju Bobby George (Aug. 2003)
47. The first woman Chairman and Managing Director of NABARD — Mrs. Ranjana Kumar
48. The highest individual test scorer of India — Virendra Sehwag (309 runs in the first test in Multan against Pakistan)
49. The first Indian cricketer to make double centuries five times — Rahul Dravid (playing test against Pakistan in Pakistan in April 2004)
50. The first Odisha woman to top I.A.S. — Smt. Roopa Mishra (Indian Civil Services Exam., 2003).

51. The first Sikh Prime Minister of India — Dr. Manmohan Singh
52. The first woman Director General of Police of a State — Kanchan C. Bhattacharya (DGP Uttarakhand
53. The first woman to be appointed as the crime branch chief — Meera Borwankar (took over as crime branch chief of Mumbai police)
54. The first woman to reach the rank of Lt. General in the Indian army — Puneeta Arora (Commandant, Armed Forces Medical College, Pune)
55. The first Indian to cross seven important seas by swimming — Bula Chaudhury
56. The first woman to become Indian Air Force's first woman Air Marshal —Padma Bandhopadhyay
57. The first youngest MP, at the age of 25 years —Dharmendra Yadav (Mainpuri : Samajwadi Party)
58. India's first woman athlete to win WTA Open Tennis title —Sania Mirza (Feb. 2005, Hyderabad)
59. The first Indian to set a world record of ever having reached the heighest of heights yet in a hot balloon. —Vijaypath Singhania (Nov. 26, 2005. 69852 ft.)
60. The first wonder child of Odisha only about 4 years and a half of age completes a race of 65 km —Budhia (May 2006)
61. The first woman Commissioner of Police of an Indian metro (Chennai Metro Police) — Letika Saran
62. The first Indian to Ski to the North Pole — Ajeet Bajaj (April 26, 2006)
63. The first woman President of the Republic of India —Pratibha Patil
64. The first former member of Parliament to be awarded death sentence by a local court for murder — Anand Mohan (Oct. 3, 2007 in District Magistrate Gopalganj murder case)
65. India's first sportsman who honoured India by winning gold in shooting at the Beijing Olympic Games in August 2008 —Abhinav Bindra
66. The first woman speaker of the Lok Sabha —Meira Kumar (Elected on June 3, 2009)
67. The first woman head of state to fly in a frontline fighter aircraft —Ms. Pratibha Patil, President of India
68. The first Indian origin school girl to be crowned as America's teen Queen —Anysha Panesar
69. The first Indian woman to cross Gobi desert —Sucheta Kadethanker
70. India's first tribal President —Droupadi Murmu (July 2022)
71. SEBI first women chairperson —Madhabi Puri Buch (Feb. 2022)
72. First Women Director General of Council of Scientific and Industrial Research (CSIR) —Dr. N. Kalaiselvi (Aug. 2022)

First in the World

1. Chairman of Peoples Republic of China —Mao-Tse-Tung
2. President of the Chinese Republic —Dr. Sun Yat Sen
3. President of U.S.A. —George Washington
4. Chinese Traveller to India —*Fahein*
5. Foreign Invader to *India* —Alexander the Great
6. Person to reach South Pole —Amundsen
7. Person to reach North Pole —Robert Pearey

8. Person in Space — Yuri Gagarin
9. Person on Moon — Neil Armstrong
10. Lady to climb Mount Everest — Junko Taibei
11. European to visit China — Marco Polo
12. Place where atom bomb was dropped — Hiroshima
13. Man to walk in Space — Alexei Leonov
14. Woman cosmonaut in Space — Valentina Tereshkova
15. Woman Prime Minister of a country — Mrs. Srimavo Bhandarnaike
16. Woman President of a country — Maria Estela Peron
17. Woman to Command a Space Mission — Colonel Eileen Collins (U.S.A.)
18. The first residents of International Space station — Bill Shepherd (USA), Yuri Gidzanko and Sergei Krikalev (Russia)
19. The first blind man to scale Mt. Everest — Erik Weihenmayer (USA, May 25, 2001)
20. The first Muslim woman to become the Secretary General of Amnesty International — Irine Zubeida Khan
21. The first space astronaut to go into space seven times till date — Jerry Ross (U.S.A.)
22. The first South African to become the second space tourist — Mark Shuttleworth
23. The first woman Prime Minister of South Korea — Ms. Chang Sang
24. The first youngest grandmaster of the world in chess — Sergey Karjakin (Ukraine)
25. The first adventurer flying successfully across the English Channel without aircraft — Felix Baumgartner (July 2003)
26. China's first man in space — Yang Liwei
27. The first Muslim woman to receive Nobel Prize — Shirin Ebadi (Nobel Peace Prize 2003)
28. The woman with the highest individual Test score making a new world record—Kiran Baloch (Pakistani cricketer, scoring 242 runs playing women's cricket test against West Indies in Karachi in March, 2004)
29. The first woman of the world to climb Mt. Everest four times — Lakpa Sherpa (Nepali)
30. The first woman to cross seven important seas of the world by swimming — Bula Chaudhury (India)
31. The first aircraft pilot to round the entire world non-stop by his 2 engine aircraft in 67 hours — Steve Fossett (March 2005)
32. The first woman to be appointed as a Governor of a province in Afghanistan — Habiba Sorabhi
33. The first woman of the world to swim across five continents — Bula Chaudhury (India) (April 2005)

34. The first woman athlete to touch 5·0 metre mark in pole vault —Ms. Yelena Isinbayeva (Russian, July 2005)
35. The first Hindu Chief Justice of Pakistani Supreme Court —Justice Rana Bhagwan Das (Took over on Sept. 2, 2005 as Acting Chief Justice)
36. The first duly elected woman President of an African country —Allen Johnson Sirleaf (elected President of Liberia in Nov. 2005)
37. The first woman Governor of the State Bank of Pakistan —Shanshad Akhtar (Appointed in Dec. 2005)
38. The first woman Chancellor of Germany —Angela Merkel (Took over in Nov. 2005)
39. The first woman President of Chile —Dr. Michelle Bachelet
40. The first woman Prime Minister of Jamaica —Portia Simpson Miller (Feb. 2006)
41. The first woman foreign Secretary of England — Margaret Backett (May 2006)
42. The first double amputee to scale Mt. Everest — Mark Inglis (May 15, 2006)
43. The first woman President of the republic of India — Pratibha Patil
44. The first athlete who won eight gold medals in individual events in one Olympic Games —Michael Phelps (U.S.A.) won eight medals in swimming at Beijing Olympiad, 2008
45. The first batsman who scored double century in One Day International Cricket —Sachin Tendulkar
46. The first woman cricketer who scored century in Twenty-20 International match — Deand Dottin
47. The first person with amputated arms and legs to swim across the English channel —Philippe Croizon of France achieved the feat in September 2010
48. The First women Prime Minister of France —Elisabeth Borne (May 2022)
49. The First Women Prime Minister of Italy —Giorgia Meloni (Oct., 2022)
50. The First Women President of Slovenia —Natasa Pirc Musar (Nov. 2022)

Presidents of India

1.	Dr. Rajendra Prasad (1884–1963)	Jan. 26, 1950 to May 13, 1962
2.	Dr. S. Radhakrishanan (1888–1975)	May 13, 1962 to May 13, 1967
3.	Dr. Zakir Hussain (1897–1969)	May 13, 1967 to May 3, 1969
4.	V.V. Giri (1894–1980) (Acting)	May 3, 1969 to July 20, 1969
5.	Justice M. Hidayatullah (1905–1992) (Acting)	July 20, 1969 to Aug. 24, 1969
6.	V.V. Giri (1894–1980)	Aug. 24, 1969 to Aug. 24, 1974
7.	Fakhuruddin Ali Ahmed (1905–1977)	Aug. 24, 1974 to Feb. 11, 1977
8.	B. D. Jatti (1912–2002) (Acting)	Feb. 11, 1977 to July 25, 1977
9.	*Neelam Sanjiva Reddy (1913–1996)*	July 25, 1977 to July 25, 1982
10.	Giani Zail Singh (1913–1994)	July 25, 1982 to July 25, 1987

11.	R. Venkatraman (1910–2009)	July 25, 1987 to July 25, 1992
12.	Dr. Shankar Dayal Sharma (1918–1999)	July 25, 1992 to July 25, 1997
13.	Dr. K. R. Narayanan (1921–2005)	July 25, 1997 to July 25, 2002
14.	Dr. A.P.J. Abdul Kalam (1931–2015)	July 25, 2002 to July 25, 2007
15.	Pratibha Patil (1934–)	July 25, 2007 to July 25, 2012
16.	Pranab Mukherjee (1935–2020)	July 25, 2012 to July 25, 2017
17.	Ram Nath Kovind (1945–)	July 25, 2017 to July 25, 2022
18.	Droupadi Murmu (1958–)	July 25, 2022 to till date

Vice-Presidents of India

1.	Dr. S. Radhakrishnan (1888–1975)	(1952–57)
2.	Dr. S. Radhakrishnan (1888–1975)	(1957–62)
3.	Dr. Zakir Hussain (1897–1969)	(1962–67)
4.	V. V. Giri (1894–1980)	(1967–69)
5.	G.S. Pathak (1896–1982)	(1969–74)
6.	B.D. Jatti (1912–2002)	(1974–79)
7.	Mohd. Hidyatullah (1905–1992)	(1979–84)
8.	R. Venkatraman (1910–2009)	(1984–87)
9.	Dr. S.D. Sharma (1918–1999)	(Sept. 3, 1987 to July 25, 1992)
10.	K.R. Narayanan (1921–2005)	(Aug. 20, 1992 to July 25, 1997)
11.	Krishna Kant (1927–2002)	(Aug. 21, 1997 to July 27, 2002)
12.	Bhairon Singh Shekhawat (1924–2010)	(Aug. 19, 2002 to Aug. 11, 2007)
13.	Md. Hamid Ansari (1937–)	(Aug. 11, 2007 to Aug. 10, 2012)
14.	Md. Hamid Ansari	(Aug. 11, 2012 to Aug. 11, 2017)
15.	Venkaiah Naidu (1947–)	(Aug. 11, 2017 to August 10, 2022)
16.	Jagdeep Dhankhar (1951–)	(Aug. 11, 2022 to till date)

Prime Ministers of India

1.	Jawahar Lal Nehru (1889–1964)	Aug. 15, 1947-May 27, 1964
2.	Guljari Lal Nanda (1898–1998) (Acting)	May 27, 1964—June 9, 1964
3.	Lal Bahadur Shastri (1904–1966)	June 9, 1964—Jan. 11, 1966
4.	Guljari Lal Nanda (1898–1998) (Acting)	Jan. 11, 1966—Jan 24, 1966
5.	Indira Gandhi (1917–1984)	Jan. 24, 1966—March 24, 1977
6.	Morarji Desai (1896–1995)	March 24, 1977-July 28, 1979
7.	Charan Singh (1902–1987)	July 28, 1979—Jan. 14, 1980
8.	Indira Gandhi (1917–1984)	Jan. 14, 1980—Oct. 31, 1984
9.	Rajiv Gandhi (1944–1991)	Oct. 31, 1984–Dec.2. 1989
10.	V.P. Singh (1931–2008)	Dec. 2, 1989–Nov.9, 1990
11.	Chandra Shekhar (1927–2007)	Nov. 10, 1990–June 21, 1991
12.	P.V. Narsimha Rao (1921–2004)	June 21,1991–May15,1996
13.	A.B. Vajpayee (1924–2018)	May 16, 1996–May 31,1996

14.	H.D. Deve Gowda (1933–)	June 1, 1996–April 20,1997
15.	I. K. Gujral (1919-2012)	April 21, 1997–March 19, 1998
16.	A.B. Vajpayee (1924-2018)	March 19, 1998–April 17, 1999 April 17, 1999–Oct. 12, 1999 (Caretaker)
17.	A.B. Vajpayee (1924-2018)	Oct. 13, 1999–May 22, 2004
18.	Dr. Manmohan Singh (1932-)	May 22, 2004–May 26, 2014
19.	Narendra Damodardass Modi (1950-)	May 26, 2014 to date

Chief Justices of India

1.	Hari lal J. Kania	Jan. 26, 1950–Nov. 6, 1951
2.	M. Patanjali	Nov. 7, 1951–Jan. 3, 1954
3.	Meher Chand Mahajan	Jan. 4, 1954–Dec. 22,1954
4.	B.K. Mukherjee	Dec. 23, 1954–Jan.30, 1956
5.	S.R. Das	Feb. 1, 1956–Sept. 30, 1959
6.	B.P. Sinha	Oct. 1, 1959–Jan. 31, 1964
7.	P.B. Gajendragadkar	Feb.1, 1964–March 15, 1966
8.	A.K. Sarkar	March 16, 1966–June 29, 1966
9.	K. Subbarao	June 30, 1966–April 11, 1967
10.	K.N. Wanchoo	April 12, 19 67–Feb. 24, 1968
11.	M. Hidayatullah	Feb. 25, 1968–Dec. 16, 1970
12.	J.C. Shah	Dec. 17, 1970–Jan. 21, 1971
13.	S.M. Sikri	Jan. 22, 1971–April 25, 1973
14.	A. N. Ray	April 26, 1973–Jan. 27, 1977
15.	M.H. Beig	Jan. 28, 1977–Feb. 21, 1978
16.	Y.V. Chandrachud	Feb. 22, 1978–July 11, 1985
17.	P.N. Bhagvati	July 12, 1985–Dec. 21, 1986
18.	R.S. Pathak	Dec. 21, 1986–June 18, 1989
19.	E.S. Venkataramaiah	June 19, 1989–Dec. 18, 1989
20.	S.S. Mukherjee	Dec. 18,1989–Sept. 25, 1990
21.	Rang Nath Mishra	Sept. 26, 1990–Nov. 24, 1991
22.	K.N. Singh	Nov. 25, 1991–Dec. 12, 1991
23.	M.H. Kania	Dec. 13, 1991–Nov. 17,1992
24.	Lalit Mohan Sharma	Nov. 18, 1992–Feb. 11,1993
25.	Venkat Challiah	Feb. 12, 1993–Oct. 24, 1994
26.	Aziz Mushabber Ahmadi	Oct. 25, 1994–March 24, 1997
27.	J.S. Verma	March 25, 1997–Jan. 17, 1998
28.	M.M. Punchhi	Jan. 18, 1998–Oct. 9, 1998

29.	A.S. Anand	Oct. 10, 1998–Oct. 31, 2001
30.	S. P. Bharucha	Nov. 1, 2001–May 5, 2002
31.	B. N. Kirpal	May 6, 2002–Nov. 7, 2002
32.	G. B. Pattnaik	Nov. 8, 2002–Dec. 18, 2002
33.	V. N. Khare	Dec. 19, 2002 to May 2, 2004
34.	S. Rajendra Babu	May 2 to June 1, 2004
35.	Ramesh Chandra Lahoti	June 1, 2004 to Oct. 31, 2005
36.	Y. K. Sabharwal	Nov. 1, 2005 to Jan. 13, 2007
37.	K. G. Balakrishnan	Jan. 14, 2007 to May 12, 2010
38.	Sarosh Homi Kapadia	May 12, 2010 to Sep. 29, 2012
39.	Altamas Kabir	Sep. 29, 2012 to July 19, 2013
40.	P. Sathasivam	July 19, 2013 to April 26, 2014
41.	R. M. Lodha	April 27, 2014 to Sep. 27, 2014
42.	H. L. Dattu	Sep. 28, 2014 to Dec. 2, 2015
43.	T. S. Thakur	Dec.3, 2015 to Jan. 3, 2017
44.	J. S. Khehar	Jan.4, 2017 to Aug. 27, 2017
45.	Deepak Misra	Aug. 28, 2017 to Oct. 2, 2018
46.	Ranjan Gogoi	Oct. 3, 2018 to Nov. 17, 2019
47.	Sharad Arvind Bobde	18 Nov., 2019 to April 24, 2021
48.	N. V. Ramana	April 24, 2021 to Aug., 26, 2022
49.	Uday Umesh Lalit	Aug. 26, 2022 to Nov. 8, 2022
50.	D. Y. Chandrachud	Nov. 9, 2022 to 10 Nov., 2024
51.	Sanjiv Khanna	11 November, 2024 to till date

Chief Election Commissioners of India

1.	Sukumar Sen	March 21, 1950 to Dec. 19,1958
2.	K.V.K. Sundaram	Dec. 20, 1958 to Sept. 30, 1967
3.	S.P. Sen Verma	Oct. 1, 1967 to Sept. 30, 1972
4.	Dr. Nagendra Singh	Oct. 1, 1972 to Feb. 6, 1973
5.	T. Swaminathan	Feb. 7, 1973 to June 17, 1977
6.	S. L. Shakdhar	June 18, 1977 to June 17, 1982
7.	R. K. Trivedi	June 18, 1982 to Dec. 31, 1985
8.	R. V. S. Perishastri	Jan. 1, 1986 to Nov. 25, 1990
9.	Smt. V. S. Rama Devi (Acting)	Nov. 26, 1990 to Dec. 11,1990
10.	T. N. Sheshan	Dec. 12, 1990 to Dec. 11, 1996
11.	Dr. M. S. Gill	Dec. 12, 1996 to June 13, 2001
12.	J. M. Lyngdoh	June 14, 2001 to Feb. 6, 2004
13.	T. S. Krishnamurti	Feb. 7, 2004 to May 16, 2005
14.	B. B. Tandon	May 16, 2005 to June 29, 2006

15.	N. Gopalswami	June 29, 2006 to April 20, 2009
16.	Navin Chawla	April 20, 2009 to July 30, 2010
17.	S. Y. Quraishi	July 30, 2010 to June 10, 2012
18.	V. S. Sampath	June 11, 2012 to Jan. 14, 2015
19.	Hari Shankar Brahma	Jan. 15, 2015 to April 18, 2015
20.	Naseem Zaidi	April 19, 2015 to July 5, 2017
21.	Achal Kumar Joti	July 6, 2017 to Jan. 22, 2018
22.	Om Prakash Rawat	Jan. 23, 2018 to Dec. 2, 2018
23.	Sunil Arora	Dec. 2, 2018 to April 12, 2021
24.	Sushil Chandra	April 13, 2021 to May 14, 2022
25.	Rajiv Kumar	May 15 , 2022 to till date

Commander-in-Chiefs of India

1.	General Roy Bucher	Jan. 1, 1948-Jan. 14, 1949
2.	General K. M. Kariappa	Jan. 15, 1949–Jan. 14, 1953
3.	General Maharaj Rajendra Sinhji	Jan. 15, 1953–March 31, 1955
4.	First Marshal of the Indian Air Force	Arjan Singh

First Chiefs of Staff of Indian Forces

1.	General Maharaj Rajendra Sinhji (Army Staff)	April 1, 1955–May 14, 1955
2.	Vice Admiral R. D. Katari (Naval Staff)	April 22, 1958–June 4, 1962
3.	Air Marshal Sri Thomas Elmherst (Air Staff)	Aug. 15, 1947–Feb. 21, 1950

Chief of Defence Staff

1.	General Bipin Rawat	1 January, 2020 to 8 December, 2021
2.	Anil Chauhan	30 September, 2022 to till date

Length of Some Important Indian Rivers

Name of the River	Length (km)	
1. Indus	2,900	(In Pak & India Both)
2. Brahmaputra	2,900	(In China, India & Bangladesh)
3. Ganga	2,525	(In India Only)
4. Godavari	1,465	– do –
5. Narmada	1,312	– do –
6. Krishna	1,401	– do –
7. *Mahanadi*	*815*	– do –
8. Cauvery	800	– do –

Major Religious Populations and Persuasions (2011)

Religion	Population (Crore)	% Share in Total Population	Growth Rate
Hindu	96·63	79·8 %	16·8%
Muslim	17·22	14·2%	24·6%
Christian	2·78	2·3%	15·5%
Sikh	2·08	1·7%	8·4%
Buddhist	0·84	0·7%	6·1%
Jain	0·45	0·4%	5·4%
Other Religions & Persuasions (ORP)	0·79	0·7%	
Religion Not Stated	0·29	0·2%	

OBJECTIVE TYPE QUESTIONS

GENERAL KNOWLEDGE

Three or more answers are given against each question. To answer a question, put a mark against the only one correct answer.

Example : In order to ensure the safety of endangered species of wild life, 'Project Tiger' was started by Government of India. To start with which National Park was chosen ?

(a) Bandhavgarh National Park, Shahdol (M.P.)
(b) Gir National Park, Junagarh (Gujarat)
(c) Palamau Tiger Sanctuary, Daltonganj (Jharkhand)
(d) Corbett National Park (Uttarakhand)

The Answer is (d).

Similarly, find out the correct answer out of the alternatives given against each of the following :

1. Who among the following has been honoured with Indira Gandhi Prize for Peace, disarmament and development in 2024 ?
   (a) Today Press (b) Michelle Bachelet
   (c) Mamta Kalia (d) Vishnu Nagar

2. 34th Saraswati Samman 2024 Award was conferred to—
   (a) Geeta Press (b) Robert Mwanga
   (c) Janlow (d) Sadhu Bhadreshdas

3. The Davis Cup (2024) was won by—
   (a) Russia (b) Ukraine
   (c) Italy (d) Australia

4. The Indian Space Research Organisation (ISRO) launched the 'Chandrayaan-3' on July 14, 2023. Which of the following statements is/are correct ?
   1. ISRO Renames GSLV-MK3 as LVM3 M4 rocket which carried Chandrayaan-3.
   2. Chandrayaan-3 landed successfully on South Pole of moon 23 August, 2023.

3. Chandrayaan-3 lander was 'Vikram' and Rover was 'Pragyan'.
4. India is fourth country which now joins the US, Russia and China as only countries successfully landed an Lunar Surface.

Correct code is—

(a) Only 1 (b) Only 2
(c) Only 3 and 4 (d) All of these

5. Which team won the 9th FIFA Women's World Cup 2023 ?
(a) France (b) Spain
(c) Morocco (d) Croatia

6. Who has won the Lokmanya Tilak National Award 2024 ?
(a) Ryan Clarke (b) Avani Jaiswal
(c) Arun Raste (d) Sudha Murty

7. Which one of the following countries made an exit from Kyoto Protocol ?
(a) France (b) India
(c) Canada (d) China

8. Who has been honoured with the Dada Saheb Phalke Award in 2024 ?
(a) Wahida Rahman (b) Shashi Kapoor
(c) Shahrukh Khan (d) Dharmendra

9. The G-20 Summit 2025 will be held in—
(a) Riyadh (b) Singapore
(c) Johannesburg (d) Bali (Indonesia)

10. Who among the following is the present (June 2025) Chairman of FICCI ?
(a) Harsha Vardhan Agarwal (b) Ranjana Desai
(c) R.S. Sharma (d) Dilip Modi

11. Match the following—

(A) Steppes — 1. Temperate Grass Lands of Africa
(B) Prairies — 2. Temperate Grass Lands of South Australia
(C) Pampas — 3. Temperate Grass Lands of South America
(D) Downs — 4. Temperate Grass Lands of North America
(E) High Velds — 5. Temperate Grass Lands of Europe & Asia

	(A)	(B)	(C)	(D)	(E)
(a)	5	4	3	2	1
(b)	5	3	4	1	2
(c)	4	5	3	1	2
(d)	4	3	2	1	5

12. On May 30, 2024, Slovakia and which country signed the Artemis Accords for peaceful lunar exploration ?
(a) America (b) Thailand
(c) South Africa (d) Peru

13. What was the theme of G-20 Summit that was held in November 2024 ?
(a) Embrace
(b) Digit All
(c) Building a Just world and a Sustainable Planet
(d) Solutions to Plastic Pollution

14. The Third Battle of Panipat was fought between—
(a) The Mughals and Shershah Suri
(b) The British and the Marahattas
(c) Ahmad Shah Abdali and the Marahattas
(d) The British and the French

15. Who is the author of the book 'The Winner's Mindset' ?
(a) Lalkrishna Advani (b) Shyam Bhatia
(c) C. Raja Mohan (d) Shane Watson

16. What is the significance of Oct. 24, 1945 in world history ?
(a) The Second World War came to an end
(b) Suez Canal was nationalised
(c) First Atom Bomb was dropped on Hiroshima
(d) The United Nations Organisation was founded

17. Who has authored 'Great Soul : Mahatma Gandhi and his struggle with India' ?
(a) Aryaman Dalmiya (b) Harry Floyed
(c) Joseph Lelyveld (d) Jawahar Lal Nehru

18. The first Railway in India was started during the period of—
(a) Lord Dalhousie (b) Lord Hastings
(c) Lord Cornwallis (d) Lord Canning

19. What is studied in Mycology ?
(a) Algae (b) Fungi
(c) Ecology (d) Virus

20. What is the name of most illustrious king in the Mughal dynasty ?
(a) Chandra Gupta Maurya (b) Akbar
(c) Babar (d) Aurangzeb

21. Who has been appointed as the Vice-Chairman of NITI Aayog recently ?
(a) Suneet Sharma
(b) Suman K. Bery
(c) V.K. Yadav
(d) Ashwani Lohani

22. India has acquired the anti-Missile Technology 'Barak' from which country ?
(a) Russia
(b) USA
(c) Israel
(d) Germany

23. In which country is the 'Mongla Port', which was in the news recently, located ?
(a) Japan
(b) Bangladesh
(c) Afghanistan
(d) Iran

24. Indian Standard Time is in advance of the Greenwich Mean Time exactly by—
(a) Three hours
(b) Five and a half hours
(c) Seven hours
(d) Eight and a half hours

25. The Nobel Prize for Peace 2024 was conferred to—
(a) Ales Bialiatski
(b) K. John
(c) Center for Civil Liberties
(d) Nihon Hidankyo

26. When is 'National Space Day' celebrated every year ?
(a) 10th July
(b) 23rd August
(c) 11th June
(d) 4th November

27. Which of the following terms are/is associated with the banking sector ?
I. CBS
II. SWIFT
III. Letter of credit
IV. MCLR

Correct code is—
(a) Only I and IV
(b) Only I and III
(c) I, II and III
(d) I, II, III and IV

28. Who won the Australian Open Tennis Women's singles titles of 2025 ?
(a) Venus Williams
(b) Li Na
(c) Medison Keys
(d) Amelie Mauresmo

29. In which year did Akbar establish 'Ibadat Khana' ?
(a) 1562 AD
(b) 1575 AD
(c) 1572 AD
(d) 1582 AD

30. Which of the following is the largest alternative source of energy ?
(a) Atomic Energy (b) Geo-thermal Energy
(c) Tidal Energy (d) Solar Energy

31. Which Amendment of the Constitution of India has fixed the size of Council of Ministers at 15% of the total strength of the Lower House of the Lok Sabha and the State Legislatures ?
(a) 85th Amendment Act (b) 86th Amendment Act
(c) 91st Amendment Act (d) 84th Amendment Act

32. Which Amendment to the Constitution of India added Maithili, Dogri, Bodo and Santhali Languages in the 8th Schedule of the Constitution ?
(a) 91st (b) 92nd
(c) 90th (d) 89th

33. Which of the following is a monetary policy tool ?
(a) Open Market Operations (b) Depreciation
(c) Primary Deficit (d) Revenue Deficit

34. Who among the following has won the French Open 2024 men's singles title ?
(a) Novak Djokovic (b) Marcelo Arevalo
(c) Alexander Zverev (d) Carlos Alcaraz

35. Who won Silver medal in Paris Olympics (2024) ?
(a) Saina Nehwal (b) Neeraj Chopra
(c) Gagan Narang (d) P.V. Sindhu

36. PM Gati Shakti National Plan was launched by the Prime Minister on ...... at New Delhi.
(a) October 13, 2021 (b) January 1, 2021
(c) April 14, 2021 (d) May 13, 2021

37. The Judges of the Supreme Court of India hold office till they attain the age of—
(a) 60 years (b) 65 years
(c) 62 years (d) 63 years

38. Largest exporter of Tea in the world is—
(a) Myanmar (b) China
(c) India (d) Sri Lanka

39. A flying bird–the logo of twitter has been changed as—
(a) Y (b) ₹
(c) $ (d) X

40. The Nobel Prize for Literature for 2024 was conferred on—
(a) Saul Perlmutter (b) Brian P. Schmidt
(c) Adam G. Riess (d) Han Kang

41. The Strait of Hormuz is an important route for international traffic between—
(a) The Persian Gulf and the Gulf of Oman
(b) The Indian Ocean and the Pacific Ocean
(c) The Atlantic Ocean and the Mediterranean Sea
(d) None of the above

42. Recently India, Japan, European Union, United States and which country have launched Biopharmaceutical Alliance ?
(a) Bangladesh (b) China
(c) South Korea (d) Russia

43. What is the lowest commissioned rank in the Indian Air Force?
(a) Wing Commander (b) Flying Officer
(c) Flt. Lieutenant (d) None of these

44. Where is the Lal Bahadur Shastri National Academy of Administration ?
(a) New Delhi (b) Hyderabad
(c) Mussoorie (d) Ahmedabad

45. Name the person who demarcated the boundary line between India and Pakistan—
(a) Lord Radcliffe (b) Lord Mountbatten
(c) Lord Attlee (d) Stafford Cripps

46. By 2050, Nuclear Power is expected to provide what per cent of the country's electricity ?
(a) 15% (b) 20%
(c) 25% (d) 35%

47. Where is the headquarters of the Small Industries Development Bank of India (SIDBI) ?
(a) New Delhi (b) Kochi
(c) Lucknow (d) Mumbai

48. Who is the Present (June 2025) Chief of the Indian Army Staff ?
(a) Arun Prakash (b) S. P. Tyagi
(c) Ajit Bhavnani (d) Upendra Dwivedi

49. Recently, the Nagi and Nakati sanctuaries located in which state have been recognized as wetlands of international importance ?
(a) Bihar (b) Tamil Nadu
(c) Maharashtra (d) Himachal Pradesh

50. Where is Food Technological Research Institute ?
(a) Chennai (b) New Delhi
(c) Kanpur (d) Mysore

51. Who was the ruler of the Shishunaga dynasty, during whose reign the Second Buddhist Council was held in Vaishali ?
(a) Shishunaga (b) Nandivardhan
(c) Kalashok (d) None of these

52. The Sachar Committee which has recently submitted its report to the Union Government deals with—
(a) The Social and Economic position of backward classes
(b) Social, Economic and Educational States of the Muslim Community
(c) The position of financial adjustment between the Centre and the States
(d) The problem of Naxalism in India

53. A 'light year' is the distance equal to—
(a) $9 \cdot 46 \times 10^{15}$ metres (b) 10×10^{15} km
(c) $2 \cdot 64 \times 10^{14}$ metres (d) $1 \cdot 6 \times 10^{20}$ metres

54. Who is Present (June 2025) Chief of the Air Force ?
(a) B. B. Tondon (b) A.P. Singh
(c) S. Y. Quraishi (d) Naveen Chawla

55. Who has recently launched a mobile app called 'Sarathi 2·0' ?
(a) RBI (b) IRDA
(c) SEBI (d) NPCI

56. The source of iron-ore for Bhilai Steel Plant is—
(a) Umaria (b) Korba
(c) Dalli-Rajhara (d) Rajnandgaon

57. Forward Market Commission (FMC) has stopped trading on Saturdays for—
(a) Only agriculture commodities
(b) Only non-agriculture commodities
(c) Both (a) and (b)
(d) None of the above

58. The Government of India has formed a new command of the army known as South-Western Command with its headquarters at Jaipur. With this the number of commands of the Indian land army will be raised to—
(a) 6 (b) 8
(c) 7 (d) 5

59. Who has been recently, appointed as the new 'Deputy National Security Advisor' ?
(a) Ajit Doval (b) Anand Dubey
(c) T. V. Ravichandran (d) Rajinder Khanna

60. 52nd Chief Justice of India is—
(a) K. G. Balakrishnan (b) N.V. Ramana
(c) Gyan Sudha Misra (d) B. R. Gavai

61. Who among the following has been named Times's 2024 Person of the Year ?
(a) Volodymyr Zelensky (b) The Spirit of Ukraine
(c) Donald Trump (d) None of the above

62. Who has been honoured with 2025 Abel Prize ?
(a) Moonmoon Sen (b) Masaki Kashiwara
(c) Mantra Shanker (d) Tessy Thomas

63. 20th World Athletics Championships will be held in September 2025 at—
(a) Abuja (Nigeria) (b) Nairobi (Kenya)
(c) Tokyo (Japan) (d) Canberra (Australia)

64. Where is the headquarters of the World Health Organisation ?
(a) Paris (b) Geneva
(c) Rome (d) New York

65. Vikram Sarabhai Space Centre is located at—
(a) Bengaluru (b) Sriharikota
(c) Thiruvananthapuram (d) Trombay

66. Who became the first Indian woman cadet to receive the 'Sword of Honour' ?
(a) Vinita Singh (b) Divya Ajith Kumar
(c) Babita Kumari (d) Neelam Singh

67. Who is the First Woman in the World in to a record 4 months stay in space ?
(a) Sunita Williams (b) Isha Ambani
(c) Rachel Ken (d) None of these

68. Newly constituted private bank 'Bandhan Bank' has its headquarter at—
(a) Pune (b) Bengaluru
(c) Kolkata (d) Hyderabad

69. Of the following inventions/discoveries the one which does not pair correctly with its inventor is—
(a) Printing Press — Gutenburg
(b) Television — *J. L. Baird*
(c) Seismograph — Swinton
(d) Microscope — Janssen

70. The 2024-25 Ranji Trophy was won by—
(a) Vidarbha (b) Uttar Pradesh
(c) West Bengal (d) Delhi

71. The ICC T-20 World Cup Cricket 2024 was won by—
(a) Sri Lanka (b) India
(c) South Africa (d) New Zealand

72. Electron was discovered by—
(a) Rutherford (b) Bohr
(c) J. J. Thomson (d) Ramsay

73. Recently, the joint military exercise 'Maitri' has started between the armies of India and which country ?
(a) Afghanistan (b) Thailand
(c) The United States (d) None of these

74. Of the following pairs the wrong one is—
(a) Red Cross — Henry Dunant
(b) First Woman Cosmonaut — Junko Tabei
(c) Antiseptic Surgery — Lord Joseph Lister
(d) Theory of Evolution — Charles Darwin

75. Life Expectancy is the high in which of the following ?
(a) Japan (b) France
(c) New Zealand (d) Finland

76. Who is the present (June 2025) Vice-President of India ?
(a) Jagdeep Dhankhar (b) Sushil Chandra
(c) Shaktikanta Das (d) N.V. Ramana

77. Which country is called the Sugar Bowl of the World ?
(a) Indonesia (b) Cuba
(c) Egypt (d) Zanzibar

78. Recently distinguished who has been made the brand ambassador of sports brand 'Puma India' ?
(a) Riyan Parag (b) Both of the above
(c) Nitish Kumar Reddy (d) None of these

79. The Tamil Ramayana was the work of—
(a) Andal (b) Jayangondar
(c) Kamban (d) Ramanujam

80. Who has recently won the Lyon Masters Chess Championship for the 10th time ?
(a) Gukesh D
(b) Magnus Carlsen
(c) Pentala Harikrishna
(d) Vishwanathan Anand

81. According to the recent WHO report, which is the most polluted country in the world ?
(a) Russia
(b) Bangladesh
(c) India
(d) Syria

82. Parakram Day is celebrated on which date ?
(a) January 23
(b) June 24
(c) July 25
(d) July 31

83. Which country has recently launched the 'ALOS-4' satellite ?
(a) South Korea
(b) Japan
(c) China
(d) America

84. How many medals were won by Indian players in Paris Olympic 2024 ?
(a) 05
(b) 04
(c) 06
(d) 07

85. India proposes to join the European Union's Galileo Global Navigation Satellite System (GNSS). Which are the two countries outside Europe have already joined Galileo GNSS ?
(a) China and Japan
(b) Japan and S. Korea
(c) Israel and Japan
(d) China and Israel

86. Who is the Chancellor of Germany (June 2025) ?
(a) Friedrich Merz
(b) Gabriel Boric
(c) Angela Merkel
(d) Park Geun-hye

87. Where was the 75th State Level Forest Festival organized recently ?
(a) Bhopal
(b) Gangtok
(c) Imphal
(d) New Delhi

88. Recently, the National Commission for Protection of Child Rights has declared the mica mines of which state as child labour free ?
(a) Odisha
(b) Jharkhand
(c) Chhattisgarh
(d) West Bengal

89. The Nahar Wildlife *Sanctuary is located in which state ?*
(a) Rajasthan
(b) Haryana
(c) Assam
(d) Kerala

90. The 70th National Film Award (August 2024) for Best Feature Film was given to the film—
(a) Avijatrik
(b) Tanhaji : The Unsung Warrior
(c) Rocketry—The Nambi Effect
(d) Aattam

91. Who is called the Father of Scientific Socialism ?
(a) Karl Marx (b) Lenin
(c) Bukanin (d) Kropotkin

92. Name the Revolution which changed the life of peasants and workers—
(a) French Revolution (b) Russian Revolution
(c) English Revolution (d) American Revolution

93. Which Tiger Reserve has recently introduced the first advanced AI system for quick detection of forest fires ?
(a) Kanha Tiger Reserve (b) Pench Tiger Reserve
(c) Manas Tiger Reserve (d) Dudhwa Tiger Reserve

94. COP-29 (United Nations Climate Change Conference) was held in ?
(a) Philadelphia (USA)
(b) St. Petersburg (Russia)
(c) Biarritz, Nouvelle-Aquitaine (France)
(d) Baku (Azerbaizan)

95. Which country recently started a new military exercise, 'Azam-e-Isteh-kam' ?
(a) Saudi Arabia (b) Afghanistan
(c) Pakistan (d) None of these

96. Who is the present UN Secretary General (June 2025) ?
(a) Antonio Guterres (b) Mohamed El Baradei
(c) Kofi Annan (d) Juan Somavia

97. Who has been appointed as the chairman and CEO of Railway Board ?
(a) Satish Kumar (b) V. K. Tripathi
(c) Anil Lahoti (d) Deepak Parekh

98. As per census of 2011 the total population of India is—
(a) 1,027,015,247 (b) 1,21,08,54,977
(c) 1,206,403,540 (d) 1,370,503,540

99. 2023-World Cup Cricket was held in—
(a) South Africa (b) India
(c) England (d) Australia

100. Which king has been called the 'Napolean of India'?
(a) Chandra Gupta Maurya (b) Samudra Gupta
(c) Pulkeshin II (d) Rajendra Chola

101. Who has recently scored the fastest double century in women's test cricket ?
(a) Sarah Taylor (b) Shefali Verma
(c) Deepti Sharma (d) Sana Mir

102. Who is the present (June 2025) Foreign Secretary of India ?
(a) Sanjeev Jain (b) Vikram Misri
(c) Sanjay Mariwal (d) Akhil Gupta

103. Who was given the 'Subhash Chandra Bose Disaster Management Award 2024' for the institutional category in January 2025 ?
(a) CRPF
(b) Hindu Yuva Vahini
(c) Indian National Centre for Ocean Information Services (INCOIS)
(d) Rashtriya Swayamsevak Sangh

104. The date of implementation of G.S.T. is—
(a) January 1, 2017 (b) January 1, 2018
(c) July 1, 2017 (d) April 1, 2019

105. The National Stock Exchange Nifty 50 is based on the performance of how many companies ?
(a) 45 (b) 50
(c) 55 (d) 65

106. Which countries of the world are referred to as BRICS ?
(a) India, Brazil, South Africa, Russia and China
(b) India, South Africa, S. Korea and Indonesia
(c) India, Brazil, Germany and Japan
(d) India, Nepal, Pakistan and Sri Lanka

107. Who was awarded the Magsaysay Award for 2024 ?
(a) Karma Phuntsho (b) Rural Doctors Movement
(c) Miyazaki Hayao (d) All of these

108. National Technology Day is observed on—
(a) May 12 (b) May 14
(c) May 11 (d) May 15

109. The UN has declared the year 2025 as the—
(a) International Year of Peace and Trust
(b) *International Year of Rice*
(c) International Year of Mountains
(d) None of the above

110. Who is World Bank President (June 2025) ?
(a) Arun Kumar (b) Ajay Banga
(c) B. K. Mitra (d) Tilak Kak

111. Neeraj Chopra won Olympic Silver medal in which game at Paris Olympic 2024 ?
(a) Wrestling (b) Boxing
(c) Javelin throw (d) Tennis

112. Who is the author of 'Without Fear : The Life and Trial of Bhagat Singh' ?
(a) Dionne Bunsha (b) Vikram Seth
(c) John Brixoe and R.P.S. Malik (d) Kuldeep Nayar

113. Namdapha Wildlife Sanctuary is located in which state ?
(a) Arunachal Pradesh (b) Jammu and Kashmir
(c) Odisha (d) Mizoram

114. Who is Director General of World Health Organisation (June 2025) ?
(a) Jongwook Lee (b) Dr. Tedros Adhanom
(c) Jacques Diouf (d) Baan Ki-Moon

115. The book 'The Seven Moons of Maali Almeida' has been written by—
(a) Sharad Pawar (b) Shehan Karunatilaka
(c) Both (a) and (b) (d) None of these

116. The 59th Jnanpith Award 2024 winner is—
(a) Gulzar (b) Rambhadracharya
(c) Vinod Kumar Shukla (d) None of these

117. Who is the Present (June 2025) Chief Minister of Karnataka ?
(a) Siddaramaiah (b) Dr. Harshwardhan
(c) D. Y. Patil (d) Sarad Yadav

118. Who is the Second Woman President of India ?
(a) Sheela Dixit (b) Droupadi Murmu
(c) Pratibha Patil (d) Uma Bharati

119. Which country has topped the recently released 'Global Peace Index 2024' ?
(a) Iceland (b) Australia
(c) Sweden (d) Ireland

120. Who among the following has been honoured with Major Dhyan Chand Khel Ratna Award 2024 ?
(a) Gukesh D. (b) Harman Preet Singh
(c) Praveen Kumar (d) All of these

Answers

1. (b)	2. (d)	3. (c)	4. (d)	5. (b)	6. (d)	7. (c)
8. (c)	9. (c)	10. (a)	11. (a)	12. (d)	13. (c)	14. (c)
15. (d)	16. (d)	17. (c)	18. (a)	19. (b)	20. (b)	21. (b)
22. (c)	23. (c)	24. (b)	25. (d)	26. (b)	27. (d)	28. (c)
29. (c)	30. (d)	31. (c)	32. (b)	33. (a)	34. (d)	35. (b)
36. (a)	37. (b)	38. (b)	39. (d)	40. (d)	41. (a)	42. (b)
43. (b)	44. (c)	45. (a)	46. (c)	47. (c)	48. (d)	49. (a)
50. (d)	51. (b)	52. (b)	53. (a)	54. (b)	55. (b)	56. (c)
57. (b)	58. (c)	59. (b)	60. (d)	61. (c)	62. (b)	63. (c)
64. (b)	65. (c)	66. (b)	67. (a)	68. (c)	69. (c)	70. (a)
71. (b)	72. (c)	73. (c)	74. (b)	75. (a)	76. (a)	77. (b)
78. (c)	79. (c)	80. (d)	81. (b)	82. (a)	83. (b)	84. (c)
85. (d)	86. (a)	87. (c)	88. (b)	89. (b)	90. (d)	91. (a)
92. (b)	93. (b)	94. (d)	95. (c)	96. (a)	97. (a)	98. (b)
99. (b)	100. (b)	101. (b)	102. (b)	103. (c)	104. (c)	105. (b)
106. (a)	107. (d)	108. (c)	109. (a)	110. (b)	111. (c)	112. (d)
113. (a)	114. (b)	115. (b)	116. (c)	117. (a)	118. (b)	119. (a)
120. (d)						

Current Topics

India Suspends the Indus Waters Treaty After the Pahalgam Terror Attack

- Following the terror attack in Pahalgam in Jammu & Kashmir, India has taken strong measures, including suspending the Indus Waters Treaty, 1960 and closing the Integrated Check Post Attari with immediate effect.

Operation Sindoor : Indian Armed Forces Carried Out Precision Strike at Terrorist Camps

The Indian Armed Forces launched 'Oeration Sindoor', hitting terrorist infrastructure in Pakistan and Pakistan-occupied Jammu & Kashmir from where terrorist attacks against India had been planned and directed. Altogether, nine (9) sites have been targeted. The military strikes were conducted by India between 1:05 AM and 1:30 AM on May 7, 2025.

India's actions have been focused, measured and non-escalatory in nature. No Pakistani military facilities were targeted. India has demonstretated considerable restraint in selection of targets and method of execution. These steps come in the wake of the barbaric Pahalgam terrorist attack in which 25 Indians and one Nepali citizen were murdered, on April 22, 2025.

The military confrontation between India and Pakistan during 'Operation Sindoor' both countries agreed to a ceasefire on 10 May, 2025.

- The Cabinet Committee on Security (CCS) reviewed the overall security situation in its meeting on April 23, 2025 and directed all forces to maintain high vigil. During the meeting, the cross-border linkages of the terrorist attack were highlighted.
- According to the Foreign Secretary Vikram Misri, Pakistani nationals are not be permitted to travel to India under the SAARC Visa Exemption Scheme (SVES) visas.
- Any SVES visas issued in the past to Pakistani nationals were deemed to be cancelled. Pakistanis in India under SVES visas were directed to leave India within 48 hours.
- Defence/Military, Naval and Air Advisors in the Pakistani High Commission in New Delhi were declared *Persona Non Grata*. India withdrew its own Defence/Navy/Air Advisors from the Indian High Commission in Islamabad.

- Meanwhile, authorities have identified five terrorists —including three Pakistani nationals—behind April 22, 2025, massacre of 26 tourists in Pahalgam area of Jammu and Kashmir, one of the worst terror attacks in the region in last 20 years.
- The role of Saifullah Kasuri—a deputy to Lashkar-e-Taiba chief Hafiz Saeed is under scrutiny.

> Under the Indus Waters Treaty, 1960, India has complete rights over three eastern rivers—Ravi, Beas and Sutlej. Pakistan is entitled to receive the entire flow from the three western rivers : Indus, Jhelum and Chenab. Accordingly, India's share of the water from the three eastern rivers is 40·7 billion cubic metres, or roughly 20 per cent of total flow of the Indus basin, whereas, Pakistan receives 80 per cent of the total supply of 207·2 billion cubic metres. In addition, India can use the waters from the western rivers for non-consum-ptive uses, domestic purposes, and agricultural purposes, including, irrigation purposes and power generation.

Energy Statistics India 2025

- The Energy Statistics India 2025, released by the National Statistics Office (NSO), under MoSPI, comprises key information about reserve, capacity, production, consumption and import/export of all the energy commodities (like Coal, Lignite, Petroleum, Natural Gas, Renewable Energy, etc.) of India.

Key Highlights of the Report :

- The Total Primary Energy Supply (TPES) registered a growth of 7·8% in FY2023-24, and stood at 9,03,158 KToE (Kilo Tonnes of oil Equivalent) in the corresponding year.
- As on March 31, 2024, potential for generation of renewable energy stood at 21,09,655 Megawatt. Sectoral distribution of renewable energy generation are as follows : Wind (11,63,856 Megawatt), Solar Energy (7,48,990 Megawatt) and Large Hydro (1,33,410).
- More than half of the potential for generation of renewable energy has been concentrated within the four States of India *viz*., Rajasthan (20·3%), Maharashtra (11·8%), Gujarat (10·5%) and Karnataka (9·8%).
- The installed capacity for electricity generation from renewable energy registered a CAGR of 10·36% over the years from 81,593 MW as on 31 March, 2015, to 1,98,213 MW as on 31 March, 2024.
- The gross generation of electricity from renewable energy recorded CAGR of 6·76% over the years- 2,05,608 GWH in FY2014-15 to 3,70,320 GWH during FY 2023-24.
- Per-capita consumption of energy grew from 14,682 Mega Joule/person during FY 2014-15 to 18,410 Mega Joule/person during FY 2023-24 which is a CAGR of 2·55%.

- Percentage loss due to Transmission and Distribution which was around 23% during FY 2014-15 has gone down to around 17% during FY 2023-24.
- The consumption against Industry sector has increased from 2,42,418 KToE during FY 2014-15 to 3,11,822 KToE during FY 2023-24. All other sectors like Commercial and Public service, Residential, Agriculture and Forestry have also registered a consistent growth over the periods.

NIA Secures Successful Extradition of 26/11 Mumbai Terror Attack Mastermind Tahawwur Rana

- On April 10, 2025, the National Investigation Agency (NIA), secured the extradition of Tahawwur Hussain Rana, a Canadian citizen and native of Pakistan and the mastermind of the deadly 26/11 Mumbai terror attacks.
- He was extradited by the United States of America (USA) on April 9, 2025, after his application for a stay of extradition was denied by the US Supreme Court.
- Tahawwur Rana is accused of conspiring with David Coleman Headley alias Daood Gilani and operatives of designated terrorist organisations Lashkar-e-Taiba and Harkat-ul-Jihadi Islami along with other Pakistan-based co-conspirators, to carry out the devastating terror attacks in Mumbai in 2008.
- A total of 166 persons were killed and over 238 injured in the deadly attacks. Both LeT and HUJI have been declared as terrorist organisations by the Government of India under the Unlawful Activities (Prevention) Act, 1967.
- The formal request for his extradition was made by the National Investigation Agency (NIA) in 2020.
- On 16th May, 2023, the District Court for the Central District of California had ordered his extradition. The US District Court in the Central District of California denied Rana's petition for a writ of habeas corpus on August 10, 2023.
- On August 15, 2024, the US Court of Appeals for the Ninth Circuit affirmed that decision. On January 21, 2025, the US Supreme Court denied Rana's petition for certiorari. The Secretary of State issued a warrant ordering Rana's surrender to Indian authorities. Both the district court and the Ninth Circuit denied Rana's application for a stay of extradition, and on April 7, 2025, the US Supreme Court denied Rana's application for a stay of extradition.

- On April 9, 2025, the US Marshals Service executed the Secretary's surrender warrant by surrendering Rana to Indian authorities for transportation to India.

Bhagavad Gita and Natyashastra Added to UNESCO's Memory of the World Register

- As on April 17, 2025, Manuscripts of the Bhagavad Gita and Bharat Muni's Natyashastra were among 74 new documentary heritage collections that have were added to UNESCO's Memory of the World Register, bringing the total number of inscribed collections to 570.
- The Bhagavad Gita, a sacred dialogue between Lord Krishna and Arjuna on the battlefield of Kurukshetra, forms a part of the Mahabharata.
- Comprising 700 verses across 18 chapters, the text addresses profound philosophical questions, encouraging action, selflessness and devotion.
- It synthesizes key elements from Vedic, Buddhist, Jain and Carvaka traditions, making it a cornerstone of India's intellectual and spiritual heritage.
- The Gita has been studied and translated across the globe for centuries.
- The Natyashastra, attributed to the sage Bharat Muni, is the foundational treatise on Indian performing arts, encompassing theatre, dance and music.
- It has shaped classical art traditions across centuries and remains a guiding text for artists and scholars alike.

> In May 2024, three Indian literary works, Ramcharitmanas, Panchatantra and Sahṛdayaloka-Locana, were added to UNESCO's Memory of the World Asia-Pacific Regional Register during the tenth meeting of the Memory of the World Committee for Asia and the Pacific (MOWCAP), held in Ulaanbaatar, Mongolia.

List of Important Indian Entries in the UNESCO'S Memory of the World Register

- The I.A.S. Tamil Medical Manuscript Collection (1997)
- Archives of the Dutch East India Company (2003)
- Saiva Manuscript in Pondicherry (2005)
- Rigveda (2007)
- Tarikh-E-Khandan-E-Timuriyah (2011)
- Iaghukalacakratantrarajatika (Vimalaprabha) (2011)
- *Shantinatha Charitra (2013)*
- Maitreyayvarakarana (2017)
- Gilgit Manuscript (2017)

- Abhinavgupta (940-1015 CE) : Collection of Manuscript of His Works (2023)
- First Summit Meeting of the Non-Aligned Movement Archives (2023)
- Bhagvad Gita (2025)
- Natyashastra (2025)

Archives of the Non-Aligned Movement's first summit in Belgrade, 1961, and Dutch East India Company Archives are two joint entries.

UNESCO's Memory of the World Programme

- It was launched in 1992 to preserve global documentary heritage.
- It aims to facilitate preservation of the world's documentary heritage, particularly in areas affected by conflict and/or natural disaster; enable universal access to documentary heritage worldwide; and enhance public awareness about the significant of documentary heritage among the wider public.
- It is updated every two years.

PM Narendra Modi Inaugurates Pamban Bridge, India's First Vertical Lift

- Prime Minister Narendra Modi on April 6, 2025 inaugurated the new Pamban Bridge in Rameswaram, Tamil Nadu, which is India's first vertical lift railway sea bridge.
- He also flagged off the Rameswaram-Tambaram (Chennai) Express from the new Pabman Bridge and a Coast Guard ship which passed under the bridge.

New Pamban Bridge

- Fully automatic, no need to raise it manually.
- Bridge can be raised vertically up to 17 metres.
- The bridge can also support two railway tracks, though it currently operates on a single line.
- Bridge will be uplifted in 5 minutes and closed in 3 minutes.
- Only 72·5 metres long span of the bridge is meant to allow the free passage of ships.
- Siren will ring automatically with arrival of any cargo ship.
- Lifting and downloading of the bridge will depend on movement of the air.
- The bridge neither lifted nor bring down in case of air speed is more than 50 km per hour.
- The Pamban bridge connects the town of Mandapam in mainland India with Rameswaram on Pamban Island.

- The bridge, built at a cost of ₹ 550 crore, connects Rameswaram Island to the mainland, enhancing connectivity and boosting regional development.
- It was constructed by Rail Vikas Nigam Limited (RVNL).
- Spanning 2·07 kilometers, the bridge comprises 99 spans and a 72·5-meter-long vertical lift span that can be raised up to 17 meters, allowing the smooth passage of large ships while ensuring seamless train operations.
- The bridge features stainless steel reinforcement, high-grade paint, and fully welded joints, enhancing durability while reducing maintenance requirements.
- The new Pamban Bridge replaces the original cantilever bridge constructed by the British in 1914.
- For over 108 years, the old Pamban Bridge served as a crucial link for pilgrims, tourists, and freight transport in a region often battered by cyclones and corrosive marine weather.
- Decommissioned in December 2022, the original bridge featured a Scherzer Rolling Lift span and had become increasingly difficult to maintain.
- Recognising the need for a future-ready infrastructure, the Indian government sanctioned the new vertical lift bridge in 2019.

Donald Trump Took Oath as the 47th President of USA

- Donald Trump was sworn in as the 47th President of the United States on January 20, 2025. The swearing-in ceremony was held indoors at the Capitol Rotunda in the US Capitol, Washington DC. J.D. Vance took the oath of office as Vice President of the United States.
- India was represented by S. Jaishankar, External Affairs Minister. Chinese Vice President Han Zheng, Foreign Affairs Ministers of Japan and Australia, all the living former US Presidents—Bill Clinton, George W. Bush, and Barack Obama—attended the swearing-in ceremony.
- After swearing-in as US President, he signed several executive orders, revoking 78 of Biden administration decisions, pardoning 1,500 defendants charged in the Capitol riot of January 6, 2021, allowing short-form video app TikTok to operate for 75 more days in the United States and officially renamed the Gulf of Mexico as the Gulf of America.
- He pulled US out of the Paris Climate Treaty, and also issued order for withdrawal of the USA from WHO. He signed executive orders declaring illegal immigration at the US-Mexico border a national emergency, designating criminal cartels as terrorist organizations.

- He also signed an executive order ending birthright citizenship for children whose parents lack legal status. Birthplace-based citizenship, also called *jus soli*, grants unrestricted citizenship based on place of birth. It is guaranteed by the Fourteenth Amendment of the US Constitution.

> Panama rejected Trump's vow to take back Panama Canal which was mainly built by USA between 1904 and 1914. However, after years of protest, former US President Jimmy Carter signed a treaty with Panama in 1977 to gradually give back control and Panama took full control of the canal in 1999. The 82 km long Panama Canal accounts for an estimated 2·5 per cent of global sea trade and 40 per cent of all US container traffic passing through it between the Atlantic and Pacific Oceans. Though, China does not control the canal, a Hong Kong-based corporation, CK Hutchison Holdings has operated two of the canal's ports, located on the Caribbean and Pacific entrances, since 1997.

90 Days Pause on Reciprocal Tariffs Imposed by Donald Trump

- On April 9, 2025, US President Donald Trump announced a pause of 90 days in implementing the 'Reciprocal Tariffs' on other countries except China.
- Earlier, Donald Trump while proclaiming April 2, 2025, as the 'Liberation Day,' he issued an executive order imposing a 10% baseline reciprocal tariff on nearly all US major trading partners (effective since April 5, 2025), and an additional individualized reciprocal tariff on 57 countries (ought to be effective from April 9, 2025.)

> When a country imposes import duty to match and counteract the tariffs imposed by other countries, it is known as the 'Reciprocal Tariffs.' These tariffs are meant to promote balanced trade and to protect domestic industries.

Tariffs Announced by Trump Since February 2025

- **Canada and Mexico** : On February 1, 2025, a 25% tax was imposed on exports from both the countries to the US. Import of energy from Canada was imposed 10% duty. They were exempted from 10% reciprocal baseline tariff. It eventually came into effect from March 4, 2025, after a pause of one month.
- **Product-based tariffs :** A 25% import duty on all steel and aluminium, and their products entering the US market, with effect from March 12, 2025. With effect from April 3, 2025, 25% duties on cars came into force which was announced in March, 2025.

Countries	USA Discounted Reciprocal Tariffs Announced
Cambodia	49%
Vietnam	46%
Sri Lanka	44%
Bangladesh	37%
South Korea	25%
Japan	24%
European Union	20%
United Kingdom, Brazil, Singapore, Australia	10%
Country-specific tariffs (above) were calculated by estimating how much each of these countries charges on US goods and then halving it to reach 'USA discounted reciprocal tariffs'.	

- **Tariff on China :** In February 2025, a 10% tariff was announced on Chinese goods, which have increased to 34 % and further upto 125% on April 9, 2025. In retaliation, China announced 125% tariffs on US products with effect from April 12, 2025. China also banned exports to the United States of gallium, germanium, antimony and other key high-tech materials with potential military applications. On April 15, 2025, new tariff of up to 245% on Chinese imports was announced by USA, as a part of 'America First Trade Policy.'
- **Tariff on India :** India was imposed with a 26% 'discounted reciprocal tariff', which is half of the tariff imposed by India on US. Earlier, the White House documents showed a 27% duty on India, but was later revised downwards to 26%, before imposing pause of 90 days on tariffs. But the US reciprocal tariff on India stands at 10% *i.e.*, baseline reciprocal tariff.
- On April 11, 2025, the US President Donald Trump's administration exempted smart-phones, computers and some other electronic devices from 'reciprocal' tariffs, including the 125% levies imposed on Chinese imports. The exemption was effective for products that entered the US or left warehouses starting on April 5, 2025.

●●●

UNION GOVERNMENT (INDIA)

President : Droupdi Murmu **Vice President :** Jagdeep Dhankhar

Cabinet Ministers

Narendra Modi	Prime Minister and also in-charge of : Ministry of Personnel, Public Grievances and Pensions; Department of Atomic Energy; Department of Space; All important policy issues; and All other portfolios not allocated to any Minister.
Raj Nath Singh	Minister of Defence
Amit Shah	Minister of Home Affairs; and Minister of Cooperation
Nitin Jairam Gadkari	Minister of Road Transport and Highways
Jagat Prakash Nadda	Minister of Health and Family Welfare; and Minister of Chemicals and Fertilizers
Shivraj Singh Chouhan	Minister of Agriculture and Farmers Welfare; and Minister of Rural Development
Smt. Nirmala Sitharaman	Minister of Finance; and Minister of Corporate Affairs
Dr. Subrahmanyam Jaishankar	Minister of External Affairs
Manohar Lal	Minister of Housing and Urban Affairs; and Minister of Power
H. D. Kumaraswamy	Minister of Heavy Industries; and Minister of Steel
Piyush Goyal	Minister of Commerce and Industry
Dharmendra Pradhan	Minister of Education
Jitan Ram Manjhi	Minister of Micro, Small and Medium Enterprises
Rajiv Ranjan Singh alias Lalan Singh	Minister of Panchayati Raj; and Minister of Fisheries, Animal Husbandry and Dairying
Sarbananda Sonowal	Minister of Ports, Shipping and Waterways
Dr. Virendra Kumar	Minister of Social Justice and Empowerment
Kinjarapu Rammohan Naidu	Minister of Civil Aviation
Pralhad Joshi	Minister of Consumer Affairs, Food and Public Distribution; and Minister of New and Renewable Energy
Jual Oram	Minister of Tribal Affairs
Giriraj Singh	Minister of Textiles
Ashwini Vaishnaw	Minister of Railways; Minister of Information and Broadcasting; and Minister of Electronics and Information Technology
Jyotiraditya M. Scindia	Minister of Communications; and Minister of Development of North Eastern Region
Bhupender Yadav	Minister of Environment, Forest and Climate Change
Gajendra Singh Shekhawat	Minister of Culture; and Minister of Tourism

Smt. Annpurna Devi	Minister of Women and Child Development
Kiren Rijiju	Minister of Parliamentary Affairs; and Minister of Minority Affairs
Hardeep Singh Puri	Minister of Petroleum and Natural Gas
Dr. Mansukh Mandaviya	Minister of Labour and Employment; and Minister of Youth Affairs and Sports
G. Kishan Reddy	Minister of Coal; and Minister of Mines
Chirag Paswan	Minister of Food Processing Industries
C.R. Patil	Minister of Jal Shakti

Ministers of States (Independent Charge)

Rao Inderjit Singh	Minister of State (Independent Charge) of the Ministry of Statistics and Programme Implementation; Minister of State (Independent Charge) of the Ministry of Planning; and Minister of State in the Ministry of Culture
Dr. Jitendra Singh	Minister of State (Independent Charge) of the Ministry of Science and Technology; Minister of State (Independent Charge) of the Ministry of Earth Sciences; Minister of State in the Prime Minister's Office; Minister of State in the Ministry of Personnel, Public Grievances and Pensions; Minister of State in the Department of Atomic Energy; and Minister of State in Department of Space.
Arjun Ram Meghwal	Minister of State (Independent Charge) of the Ministry of Law and Justice; and Minister of State in the Ministry of Parliamentary Affairs.
Jadhav Prataprao Ganpatrao	Minister of State (Independent Charge) of the Ministry of Ayush; and Minister of State in the Ministry of Health and Family Welfare.
Jayant Chaudhary	Minister of State (Independent Charge) of the Ministry of Skill Development and Entrepreneurship; and Minister of State in the Ministry of Education.

Ministers of State

Jitin Prasada	Minister of State in the Ministry of Commerce and Industry; and Minister of State in the Ministry of Electronics and Information Technology.
Shripad Yesso Naik	Minister of State in the Ministry of Power; and Minister of State in the Ministry of New and Renewable Energy.
Pankaj Chaudhary	Minister of State in the Ministry of Finance.
Krishan Pal	Minister of State in the Ministry of Cooperation.
Ramdas Athawale	Minister of State in the Ministry of Social Justice and Empowerment.
Ram Nath Thakur	Minister of State in the Ministry of Agriculture and Farmers Welfare.
Nityanand Rai	Minister of State in the *Ministry of Home Affairs*.
Smt. *Anupriya Patel*	*Minister* of State in the Ministry of Health and Family Welfare; and Minister of State in the Ministry of Chemicals and Fertilizers.

V. Somanna	Minister of State in the Ministry of Jal Shakti; and Minister of State in the Ministry of Railways.
Dr. Chandra Sekhar Pemmasani	Minister of State in the Ministry of Rural Development; and Minister of State in the Ministry of Communications.
Prof. S.P. Singh Baghel	Minister of State in the Ministry of Fisheries; Animal Husbandry and Dairying; and Minister of State in the Ministry of Panchayati Raj.
Sushri Sobha Karandlaje	Minister of State in the Ministry of Micro, Small and Medium Enterprises; and Minister of State in the Ministry of Labour and Employment.
Kirtivardhan Singh	Minister of State in the Ministry of Environment, Forest and Climate Change; and Minister of State in the Ministry of External Affairs.
B. L. Verma	Minister of State in the Ministry of Consumer Affairs, Food and Public Distribution; and Minister of State in the Ministry of Social Justice and Empowerment.
Shantanu Thakur	Minister of State in the Ministry of Ports, Shipping and Waterways.
Suresh Gopi	Minister of State in the Ministry of Petroleum and Natural Gas; and Minister of State in the Ministry of Tourism.
Dr. L. Marugan	Minister of State in the Ministry of Information and Broadcasting; and Minister of State in the Ministry of Parliamentary Affairs.
Ajay Tamta	Minister of State in the Ministry of Road Transport and Highways.
Bandi Sanjay Kumar	Minister of State in the Ministry of Home Affairs.
Kamlesh Paswan	Minister of State in the Ministry of Rural Development.
Bhagirath Choudhary	Minister of State in the Ministry of Agriculture and Farmers Welfare.
Satish Chandra Dubey	Minister of State in the Ministry of Coal; and Minister of State in the Ministry of Mines
Sanjay Seth	Minister of State in the Ministry of Defence.
Ravneet Singh	Minister of State in the Ministry of Food Processing Industries; and Minister of State in the Ministry of Railways.
Durgadas Uikey	Minister of State in the Ministry of Tribal Affairs.
Smt. Raksha Nikhil Khadse	Minister of State in the Ministry of Youth Affairs and Sports.
Sukanta Majumdar	Minister of State in the Ministry of Education; and Minister of State in the Ministry of Development of North Eastern Region.
Smt. Savitri Thakur	Minister of State in the Ministry of Women and Child Development.
Tokhan Sahu	Minister of State in the Ministry of Housing and Urban Affairs.

Raj Bhushan Choudhary	Minister of State in the Ministry of Jal Shakti.
Bhupathi Raju Srinivasa Varma	Minister of State in the Ministry of Heavy Industries; and Minister of State in the Ministry of Steel
Harsh Malhotra	Minister of State in the Ministry of Corporate Affairs; and Minister of State in the Ministry of Road Transport and Highways.
Smt. Nimuben Jayantibhai Bambhaniya	Minister of State in the Ministry of Consumer Affairs; Food and Public Distribution.
Murlidhar Mohol	Minister of State in the Ministry of Cooperation; and Minister of State in the Ministry of Civil Aviation.
George Kurian	Minister of State in the Ministry of Minority Affairs; and Minister of State in the Ministry of Fisheries, Animal Husbandry and Dairying.
Pabitra Margherita	Minister of State in the Ministry of External Affairs; and Minister of State in the Ministry of Textiles.

States of India, their Governors and Chief Ministers

State	***Governor***	***Chief Minister***
Andhra Pradesh	S. Abdul Nazeer	N. Chandrababu Naidu
Arunachal Pradesh	Kaiwalya Trivikram Parnaik	Pema Khandu
Assam	Lakshman Prasad Acharya	Himanta Biswa Sarma
Bihar	Arif Mohammad Khan	Nitish Kumar
Goa	P. S. Sreedharan Pillai	Pramod Sawant
Gujarat	Shri Acharya Devvrat	Bhupendra Patel
Haryana	Bandaru Dattatraya	Nayab Singh Saini
Himachal Pradesh	Shiv Prasad Shukla	Sukhvinder Singh Sukhu
Karnataka	Thaawarchand Gelhot	Siddaramaiah
Kerala	Rajendra Vishwanath Arlekar	Pinarayi Vijayan
Madhya Pradesh	Mangubhai Chhaganbhai Patel	Dr. Mohan Yadav
Maharashtra	C.P. Radhakrishnan	Devendra Fadnavis
Meghalaya	C.H. Vijayshankar	Conrad Sangma
Manipur	Ajay Kumar Bhalla	President's Rule
Mizoram	Gen. (Dr.) V.K. Singh	Lalduhawma
Nagaland	La. Ganeshan	Neiphiu Rio
Odisha	Hari Babu Kambhampati	Mohan Charan Majhi
Punjab	Gulab Chand Kataria	Bhagwant Singh Mann
Rajasthan	Haribhau Kishanrao Bagde	Bhajan Lal Sharma
Sikkim	Om Prakash Mathur	Prem Singh Tamang
Tamilnadu	R. N. Ravi	M.K. Stalin
Tripura	N. Indrasena Reddy	Manik Saha
Uttar Pradesh	Smt. Anandiben Patel	Yogi Adityanath
West Bengal	C.V. Anand Bose	Mamta Banerjee
Chhattisgarh	Raman Deka	Vishnu Deo Sai
Uttarakhand	*Lt. Gen. Gurmit Singh*	Pushkar Singh Dhami
Jharkhand	Santosh Gangwar	Hemant Soren
Telangana	Jishnu Dev Verma	Revanth Reddy

Union Territories, their Heads and Chief Ministers

Andaman and Nicobar Island	D. K. Joshi (Lieutenant Governor)	
Chandigarh	Gulab Chand Kataria (Administrator)	
Dadra and Nagar Haveli, Daman and Diu	Praful Patel (Administrator)	
Delhi*	Vinai Kumar Saxena (Lieutenant Governor)	Rekha Gupta
Lakshadweep	Prajul Patel (Administrator)	
Puducherry	K. Kailashnathan (Lieutenant Governor)	N. Rangaswamy
Jammu & Kashmir	Manoj Sinha (Lieutenant Governor)	Omar Abdullah
Ladakh	B.D. Mishra (Lieutenant Governor)	

* National Capital Territory

Important Head of Offices

Om Birla	Speaker, Lok Sabha
Gyanesh Kumar	Chief Election Commissioner
Ranjana Desai	Chairman, Press Council of India
Dr. Ajay Kumar	Chairman, U.P.S.C.
Dinesh Maheshwari	Chairman, Law Commission
Justice B. R. Gavai	The Chief Justice of India
Sanjay Malhora	Governor, Reserve Bank of India
C. S. Setty	Chairman, State Bank of India
R. Venkataramani	Attorney General of India
Satish Kumar	Chairman, Railway Board
Iqbal Singh Lalpura	Chairman, National Commission for Minorities
Ravi Agarwal	Chairman, Central Board of Direct Taxes
Dr. Ajit Kumar Mohanty	Chairman, Atomic Energy Commission
V. Narayanan	Chairman, Indian Space Research Organisation (ISRO)
Harshavardhan Agarwal	Chairman, FICCI
Dr. Mangi Lal Jat	Director General, Indian Agriculture Research Council (ICAR)
Tuhin Kanta Pandey	Chairman, SEBI
Amreshwar Pratap Sahi	President, National Consumer Disputes Redressal Commission
M. Vineet Joshi (Interim)	Chairman, University Grants Commission
Siddhartha Mohanty	Chairman, LIC

Heads and Prime Ministers of Various Countries of the World

Country	*Heads*	*Prime Ministers*
Australia	Sam Mostyn (G.G.)	Anthony Albanese
Austria	Alexander Van der Bellen (P.)	Christain Stocker
Argentina	Javier Milei (P)	—
Bangladesh	Mohd. Shahabuddin Chuppu (P.)	Muhammad Yunus (Chief Advisor)
Bhutan	Jigme Khesar Namgyal Wangchuk (K.)	Tshering Tobgay
Brazil	Luiz Inacio Lula da Silva (P.)	—
Cuba	Miguel Diaz Canel (P.)	Manuel Marrero Cruz
Canada	Mary Simon	Mark Carney
Chile	Gabriel Boric (P.)	—
China (Republic)	Xi Jinping (P.)	Li Qiang
Cambodia	Prince Norodom Sihmoni (K.)	Hun Manet
Czech Republic	Petr Pavel (P.)	Petr Fiala
Congo Repb.	Dennis Sassou Nguesso (P.)	Anatole Collinet Makosso
Denmark	King Frederik (X)	Mette Frederiksen
Egypt	Abdel Fatteh el-Sisi (P.)	Mostafa Madbouly
France	Emmanuel Macron (P.)	Francois Bayrou
Germany	Frank-Walter Steinmeier (P.)	Friedrich Merz (Chancellor)
Greece	Konstantinos Tassoulas (P.)	Kyriakos Mitsotakis
Haiti	Leslie Voltaire (P.)	Alix Didier Fils-Aime
Hungary	Tamas Sulyok (P.)	Viktor Orban
Ireland	Michael D. Higgins (P.)	Micheal Martin
Indonesia	Prabowo Subianto (P)	—
Iran	Masoud Pezeshkian	—
Israel	Issac Herzog (P.)	Benjamin Netanyhu
Iraq	Abdul Latif Rashid (P.)	Mohammed al-Sudani
Italy	Sargio Mattarella (P.)	Giorgia Meloni
Japan	Naruhito (Emperor)	Shigeru Ishiba
Jordan	Abdullah II bin Al Hussein (K.)	Jafar Hassan
Kenya	William Ruto (P.)	—
N. Korea	Kim Jong-un (P.)	—
S. Korea	Lee Jae-Myung (P.)	Han Duck-Soo.
Lebanon	Joseph Aoun (P.)	Nawaf Salam
Malaysia	Ibrahim Iskandar (K.)	Anwar Ibrahim
Maldives	Mohamed Muizzu	—
Mauritius	Dharam Gokhool	Navin Ramgoolam
Mexico	Claudia Sheinbaum Pardo (P.)	—
Morocco	Mohammed VI (K.)	Aziz Akhannouch
Namibia	Netumbo Nandi-Ndaitwah (P.)	Sara Kuugongelwa
Nepal	Ram Chandra Poudel (P.)	K.P. Sharma Oli
New Zealand	Dame Cindy Kiro (G.G.)	Christopher Luxon

Netherlands	Willem Alexander (K.)	Dick Schoof
Norway	King Herald V (K.)	Jonas Gahr Store
Pakistan	Asif Ali Zardari (P.)	Shehbaz Sharif
Philippines	Bangbong Marcos (P.)	—
Portugal	Marcelo Rebelo de Sousa (P.)	Luis Montenegro
Peru	Dina Boluarate (P.)	Eduardo Arana Ysa
Romania	Nicusor Dari (P.)	Lile Bdojan
Russia	Vladimir Putin (P.)	Mikhail Mishustin
Sweden	Carl XVI Gustaf (K.)	Ulf Kristersson
Somalia	Hassan Sheikh Mohamud	Hamza Abdi Barre
Sri Lanka	Anura Kumara DissanayaKe (P.)	Harini Amarasuriya
Syria	……………	Ahmed al-Sharaa
South Africa	Cyril Ramaphosa (P.)	—
Sudan	Abdel Fattah of Burhan (P.)	Osman Hussein
Spain	Felipe VI (K.)	Pedro Sanchez
Switzerland	Viola Amherd (P.)	—
Thailand	Maha Vajiiralongkorn (K.)	Paetongtarm Shinawatra
Tanzania	Sumia Suluhu Hassan (P.)	Kasim Majaliwa
Turkiye	Recep Tayyip Erdogan (P.)	—
U. K.	Charles III (K.)	Keir Starmer
U. S. A.	Donald Trump (P.)	—
Venezuela	Nicolas Maduro Moros (P.)	—
Zambia	Hakainde Hichilema (P.)	—
Zimbabwe	Emmerson Mnangagwa (P.)	—

Other Important Personality

Kristalina Georgieva	Managing Director, International Monetary Fund
Antonio Guterres	Secretary General, United Nations Organisation
Ajay Banga	President, World Bank
Dr. T. A. Ghebreyesus	Director General, World Health Organization
Golam Sarwar	Secretary General, SAARC
Ngozi Okonjo-Iweala	Director-Gen., World Trade Organisation

Chiefs of Indian Defence Services

Chief of the Army Staff	Gen. Upendra Dwivedi
Chief of the Air Staff	Air Chief Marshal Amar Preet Singh
Chief of the Naval Staff	Admiral Dinesh Kumar Tripathi
First Field Marshal	Gen. S. H. F. J. Manekshaw
Second Field Marshal	Gen. K. M. Kariappa
First Chief of Defence Staff	Gen. Bipin Rawat
Chief of Defence Staff	General Anil Chauhan